D0165793

GENDERED WORK

GENDERED WORK
Sexuality, family and the labour market

Lisa Adkins

Open University Press
Buckingham · Philadelphia

Open University Press
Celtic Court
22 Ballmoor
Buckingham
MK18 1XW

and
1900 Frost Road, Suite 101
Bristol, PA 19007, USA

First Published 1995

Copyright © Lisa Adkins 1995

All rights reserved. Except for the quotation of short passages for the
purpose of criticism and review, no part of this publication may be
reproduced, stored in a retrieval system, or transmitted, in any form
or by any means, electronic, mechanical, photocopying, recording or
otherwise, without the prior written permission of the publisher or a
licence from the Copyright Licensing Agency Limited. Details of
such licences (for reprographic reproduction) may be obtained from
the Copyright Licensing Agency Ltd of 90 Tottenham Court Road,
London, W1P 9HE.

A catalogue record of this book is available from the British Library

Library of Congress Cataloging-in-Publication Data
Adkins, Lisa, 1966–
    Gendered work: sexuality, family and the labour market / Lisa
Adkins.
        p.   cm.
    Includes bibliographical references and index.
    ISBN 0-335-19297-1   ISBN 0-335-19296-3 (pbk.)
    1. Sex role in the work environment – Great Britain.   2.
Women – Employment – Great Britain.   3. Sex discrimination in
employment – Great Britain.   4. Tourist trade – Social aspects –
Great Britain. I. Title.
HD6060.5.G7A34   1994
331.4'133'0941 – dc20   94-22206
                                                                CIP

Typeset by Vision Typesetting, Manchester
Printed in Great Britain by Biddles Limited, Guildford and King's Lynn

Contents

Acknowledgements

The major themes addressed and developed in *Gendered Work* originated through work for my Ph.D. at Lancaster University. During that time, and since then, a number of people have read and commented on various draft chapters and parts of chapters which now form this book. Of those people I would particularly like to thank Scott Lash, Celia Lury, Mike Savage, Betsy Stanko, Penny Tinkler, John Urry, Alan Warde, Sylvia Walby and Anne Witz. A special thanks also goes to Diana Leonard who read and gave detailed feedback on the final version of the manuscript. Finally, I would like to thank Jem Thomas and Jeffrey Weeks who, through their support at the University of the West of England, allowed me the time and space to complete the book.

1

Introduction

This book is concerned with the gendering of the contemporary labour market. That is to say, it has as its focus the processes through which power relations between men and women in employment are constituted, and how 'advantage and disadvantage, exploitation and control, action and emotion, and meaning and identity are patterned through and in terms of a distinction between male and female' (Acker 1990:146). More specifically, it explores the significance of 'sexuality' and 'the family' for this process, especially for the construction of work relations between men and women in paid work. This focus is relatively unusual because until very recently both have been accorded minimal significance in the processes and practices of gendering within the labour market; for example, both sexual and family relations have been regarded as either external, or at most peripheral to contemporary employment.

The labour market and sexuality

When I began my research for this book in the late 1980s, most labour market theory, including that produced by feminists on 'women and work' or 'gender and employment', either completely ignored sexuality or considered it unimportant for the gendered operations of the labour market. Some of this theory seemed in fact to deny that sexual, as opposed to gender, relations actually operated in the labour market, despite a great deal of feminist research which had shown just how important sexual relations are in shaping all (other) aspects of social reality for women. On the other hand, analyses of sexuality at that time mainly used frameworks which made it difficult to link the production of gender inequalities in sexuality to those of the labour market. For example, many authors saw the relations of sexuality determining all forms of gender inequality, but simply assumed, and did not specify how these relations constituted 'economic' inequalities (see Chapter 2).

Consequently, at the end of the 1980s a theoretical gap existed within feminism. 'Sexuality' and 'the labour market' were treated as completely separate areas of analysis and their intersection was rarely if ever addressed. Moreover, the frameworks which were used and developed for the analyses of each area made it difficult to consider the significance of one for the operations of the other. The frameworks used to analyse the labour market were derived for the most part from industrial sociology and political economy, and they typically gave priority to sets of economic relations in understanding the gendered operations of the labour market. This excluded the possibility of a consideration of the significance of sexual relations for such dynamics. The frameworks used to analyse sexuality were derived from social interactionism, Foucauldian discourse analysis and psychoanalysis, and they were typically concerned with understanding the formation of gendered subjectivity and identities. Such a focus generally excluded the possibility of an understanding of gendered work relations.

But while analyses of sexuality and of the labour market used fairly incongruous frameworks, each set of analyses had nevertheless established that its area of concern constituted a substantive area of gender inequality. Analysis of the labour market had shown that women typically earn less than men (e.g. Beechey 1987), participate in waged work to a lesser extent than men (e.g. Martin and Roberts 1984), have less secure employment than men (e.g. Bruegel 1986), are segregated into a limited range of occupations (e.g. Hakim 1979, 1981), are excluded from access to labour market resources (such as particular skills; e.g. Phillips and Taylor 1986) and have unequal access to promotional/career ladders *vis-à-vis* men (e.g. Kanter 1977). Feminists had, in other words, documented the operation of systematic forms of gender inequality in this domain. Equally, systematic gender inequality had been shown to structure relations of sexuality. This had been revealed in particular through studies of men's sexual violence against women, including sexual harassment, rape, assault and the threat of sexual violence (e.g. Russell 1984; Kelly 1988). These studies had established sexual violence as a central feature of gender relations and shown women's lives to be extensively controlled, both directly and indirectly, through male-dominated heterosexuality.

Despite the recognition of both sexuality and the labour market as substantive areas of gender inequality, there had been only minimal recognition of any overlap between the two, though there had been some work on the operation of sexual harassment within the labour market on how unwanted sexual attention affected women's position in employment (e.g. MacKinnon 1979; Stanko 1988). Some early feminist work on sexuality suggested that there was 'work' involved in sexuality. For example, it was said that women worked at making men feel sexually good by, for example, faking orgasms in heterosexual sex (e.g. Koedt 1970; Lyndon 1970; Whiting 1972). But although this is clearly significant in terms of a consideration of the interplay between sexuality and gendered work relations within the sphere of employment, these ideas were not fully explicated. There had also been some work on the lives of women employed in explicitly sexual forms of paid work – notably in the pornography industry and in prostitution (e.g. Barry 1979; Delacoste and Alexander 1988) – but these forms of paid work had generally been treated as quite apart or separate from the 'real' labour market by feminist labour market theorists.

While such work indicated the possibility of an overlap between the dynamics of sexuality and the labour market, in general both were treated – and continue to be treated – as if they simply co-exist and rarely meet. Even those analyses which came close to considering that they do have a relationship (e.g. studies of sexual harassment at work) generally located sexuality and the operations of the labour market in this differentiated fashion (see Chapter 2); and when analysts saw work and sexuality meeting, they saw them overlapping rather than interacting and interrelating.

Since the late 1980s, however, there has been a growing recognition that sexuality can no longer be left off the agenda when it comes to thinking about the gendering of the labour market (Hearn and Parkin 1987; Hearn et al. 1989; Pringle 1989a,

1989b; Cockburn 1991; Adkins 1992a, 1992b; Adkins and Lury 1992; Savage and Witz 1992), and there have been a number of studies which have explicitly attempted to consider the interaction between sexual and employment relations (e.g. Hearn and Parkin 1987; Pringle 1989a, 1989b; Cockburn 1991). However, as this book will show, many of these analyses have still not addressed a number of fundamental questions regarding sexuality, nor the relationship between gendered sexuality and the gendered labour market.

The labour market and the family

While sexuality and the labour market have a history of being analytically separated, the exclusion of the relations of the family from analyses of employment has followed a different track, in that a number of analyses have suggested an overlap between these sets of relations. In particular, some analyses of the family see (unpaid) work relations as central to understanding the gender (and generational) relations of family members, and show that these family production relations operate to produce both non-market and market goods and services (Delphy 1970, 1984; Finch 1983, 1989; Morris 1990; Delphy and Leonard 1992). But despite this, work relations based upon family relations are generally excluded from analyses of employment relations by feminists who focus on the labour market. The latter tend to deny the possibility of family work relations being located within the productive structure of the contemporary labour market. In Chapter 3, I show how this denial is based upon a particular account of the impact of the development of capitalism upon production for the market, which sees family work relations as distinct from, and generally dependent on, the work relations of the labour market.

The main concern of this book is to address these imbalances. It attempts to specify for particular areas of employment (1) the nature of the intersection between the apparently disparate processes of sexuality and the labour market, and (2) the relationship between aspects of family work relations and employment relations. In so doing, it sheds light on the general nature of gendered work relations within employment, especially forms of the control and exploitation of women's labour which operate in the labour market. It cannot and does not attempt to cover the significance of the whole of sexuality, the whole of the labour market or the whole of the relations of the family for the formation of gender relations. Rather, it aims to specify the nature of the intersection and interaction of sets of relations within one particular area of employment – that is, aspects of paid and unpaid work within the contemporary British tourist industry.

Recent research on tourism

Tourism is gaining increasing significance both nationally and internationally as an area of employment. In 1991, the tourist industry employed 1 in 15 of the world's paid workforce (*The Observer*, 4 August 1991). The United Nations World Tourism Organization has estimated that by the year 2000 tourism will have become the single most important global economic activity (cited in Enloe 1989: 20; and Urry 1990: 5). In Britain, the total number of people employed in tourist-related services is estimated to be between 1 and $1\frac{1}{2}$ million (Landry *et al.* 1989, Urry 1990; BTA/ETB 1993), and it has been suggested that until very recently employment within tourism was increasing at a rate of 1000 jobs per week (Williams and Shaw, cited in Urry 1990: 5).

The significance attached to tourism within both national and global economies, together with more general concerns regarding de-industrialization, the 'growth' of the service sector and the increasing recognition of the importance of leisure, consumption and consumption practices for social formations in 'late' capitalism (Bourdieu 1984; Lash and Urry 1987; Harvey 1989; Lash 1990; Urry 1990; Jameson 1991), has meant that 'tourism' and tourist practices have been the subject of some considerable research attention of late. This has resulted in some very important insights. The development and growth of tourism has been shown to be intimately connected to a range of phenomena, including western imperialism and masculinity (Enloe 1989) and formations of race, ethnicity and nationhood (Enloe 1989; Ware 1992). Similarly, the contemporary social organization of tourism, and new developments such as the de-differentiation of tourist practices from other social activities, have been linked to other wide-ranging social phenomena, including the development of new class formations (such as the rise of the service and middle classes), the development of new social movements, and changes in consumption patterns – especially those related to the rise of post-modernism and the aestheticization of consumption. (For an in-depth discussion of the connections between these social phenomena and the contemporary organization of tourism, see Urry 1990.)

A further outcome of the recent focus on tourism is that attention has turned towards the organization of work relations within its services. This in turn, like the interest in tourism in general, relates to a broader set of concerns regarding transformations within contemporary capitalist societies. In particular, the interest in tourist work relations feeds into an ongoing set of debates about the development of the service sector, the apparent increase in service activities in capitalist societies, and the nature of 'service work' (see, e.g. Gershuny and Miles 1983; Offe 1985; Walker 1985; Urry 1986). One particular area of concern within these debates has been the issue of how, or in what ways, service work (or service labour) differs from other forms of wage-labour relations. Or, to put it another way, recent research and analysis of employment in tourism has been in part concerned with the construction and specificity of 'service work'.

One important strand of such work has emphasized the ways in which 'service work' cannot be understood in terms of economic rationality alone. Offe (1985), for instance, has discussed the ways in which service labour is not only subject to economic imperatives (such as economic rationalization and standardization), but also requires that some autonomy is given to the service provider to ensure that the specific requirements or situations of customers and clients can be accommodated. Offe (1985: 105) refers to this as 'the rationality of mediation'. Service labour thus involves an element of mediation between, on the one hand, service providers and, on the other, service consumers. But Offe stresses this mediation cannot be entirely *ad hoc*. Although service activities may be orientated to the particular situations of consumers, they must also 'ultimately bring about a state of affairs which conforms to certain general rules, regulations and values' (ibid.). Thus 'service work' always has an important social function, namely the maintenance of 'normal conditions'. It is this specific 'normalizing' social role of service labour which Offe suggests distinguishes it from other forms of (wage) labour. In particular, it means that 'service work' cannot be understood in terms of economic rationality alone. What is at issue is not just fixed and clearly defined outcomes, rigid controls over work activities, and the homogenization and standardization of the labour process, but also the (re)production of the social structure.

The idea that 'service work' in general cannot simply be understood in terms of economic relations and, in particular, that the social organization of service labour is constituted in part through its 'mediating' character, can also be found in some recent analyses of the tourist industry itself. These rest on the central observation that the dynamics of tourism are structured by a specific feature of consumer services, namely the spatial and temporal proximity between production and consumption (Smith 1986; Bagguley 1987; Urry 1990). This proximity is thought to mean that cultural practices, especially the cultural expectations of consumers, act to significantly determine the social relations of production (Bagguley 1987; Urry 1990).

Urry (1990), for example, has argued that cultural relations are central to an understanding of the dynamics of tourism, including its employment relations. He argues that the latter derive their characteristics from the emphasis placed upon social interaction between producers and consumers within tourist services. This emphasis derives from the proximity of production to consumption – services for customers/clients/guests have to be delivered in the same place and at the same time as they are produced. Consequently, Urry contends, the quality of the social interaction between the provider and the consumer of the service becomes part of the product. The cultural expectations of consumers regarding service provision therefore have particular significance in structuring the form of service delivery, and hence employment relations within the industry.

This emphasis on the social interaction between the producer and consumer of the product means, according to Urry, that work relations and developments within tourism cannot simply be explained through sets of relations, particularly economic relations, internal to the industry. Rather, tourism is an industry in which work relations are significantly culturally developed: 'work in tourist industries cannot be understood separately from the cultural expectations that surround the complex delivery of such services' (Urry 1990: 41). With labour being implicated in the delivery of tourist services (that is, with part of the product being dependent upon the quality of the interaction between producers and consumers), to buy a product means 'to buy a particular social or sociological experience' (Urry 1990: 68).

On the basis of this premise, Urry goes on to distinguish two types of employees within tourist industries: those who have minimal contact with consumers, and those with a great deal of contact. Because of the specific nature of the production/consumption relationship, he believes the social composition of 'front-line' (high-contact) workers, including their social characteristics such as race, gender and age, becomes part of what is sold. Furthermore, the nature of the production/consumption process means that management intervention into areas such as employee's dress, speech and behaviour become legitimate in relation to front-line workers. Employees are encouraged and often trained to cater for consumer 'needs'. Thus service employment may often involve carrying out 'emotion work' in relation to customers (for an account of the emotional work involved in the occupation of airline stewardess, see Hochschild 1983). Urry notes that given these characteristics of front-line consumer service work, it is no coincidence that much of this work is carried out by women.

Tourism and women's employment

One of the most striking features of the constellation of consumer services (i.e. the hotels, catering and entertainment venues and the servicing jobs) which comprise Britain's (and the global) tourist industry, is the predominance of women employees (Enloe 1989). In Britain in general, employed women are disproportionately clustered in service industries. In 1991, for instance, 81 per cent of all employed women were employed in service occupations (McDowell 1991), and in 1993 in nine of the member states of the European Community,[1] more than 70 per cent of women's employment was concentrated in the service sector (European Network of Experts on the Situation of Women in the Labour Market 1993). But within the UK service industries, women are disproportionately concentrated within 'miscellaneous services' – that is, in the economic sector in which many of the major tourist services are classified (see Smith 1986). In 1981, within the hotels and catering section of the UK tourist industry, women comprised 81 per cent of waiting and bar staff, and 98 per cent of domestic staff (OPCS 1981). At present, 70 per cent of the total hotel and catering workforce are women (Crompton and Sanderson 1990: 132); and it is a sector, together with other tourist services, making an increasing contribution to Britain's total employment (see Smith 1986; Rajan 1987; Crompton and Sanderson 1990; BTA/ ETB 1993).

Research on the industry is, however, difficult. As many commentators have noted, it is an industry which relies heavily on different forms of 'non-standard' employment, including self-employment, part-time, casual and temporary employment (Dronfield and Soto 1982; Bagguley 1987: Guerrier and Lock-wood 1989; Crompton and Sanderson 1990). Many of these forms of employment are not recorded in official employment statistics and, therefore, as Crompton and Sanderson (1990) have noted in relation to the hotel and catering trade, it is difficult even to produce a precise estimate of the numbers involved, let alone to chart more long-term trends. But despite the methodological difficulties associated with 'non-standard' forms of employment, many writers have suggested that more and more women in Britain (and indeed, on a global scale) are engaged in these types of paid work (see, e.g. Mies 1986; Mitter 1986; Beechey and Perkins 1987; Westwood and Bhachu 1988; Phizacklea 1990). Given that the tourist industry is heavily dependent upon such employment, and that many of the jobs open to women in the industry constitute typical 'women's jobs', the tourist industry is an important site for researching the contemporary conditions of women's employment and the dynamics of how the labour market is and continues to be gendered.

But despite the concentration of women within many of the consumer services attached to the tourist industry, there has been relatively little attention paid to either the position of women workers within the industry or its gendered work relations. There have been studies of specific occupations, in particular of the dynamics of the exclusion and segregation of women from and within occupations (see, e.g. Guerrier 1986; on hotel managers), and some recent work has looked at the organization of women's employment in specific sections of the tourist industry, for example the hotel and catering trade (Crompton and Sanderson

1990). There has also been some research on the position of women in sex-tourism (Enloe 1989; Thoen and Kristianson 1989; Truong 1990; see also Chapter 2). But considering the very high proportion of women employed in tourist services, and just how typical the forms of employment in the industry are for women (in the form, for example, of waitressing, cleaning, bar-work and hostess work), it is surprising that there has been so little research into the gendered dynamics of tourist employment.

Conversely, the concentration of women employees in the tourist industry also raises important research questions in relation to the recent macro-analyses of 'service work', which have tended to ignore the significance of gender. Following Offe's analysis of the 'mediating' role of service work we might ask, for instance, why it is that women's labour rather than men's is implicated in service activities. Is it because women's labour plays an important role in the creation of the 'normal social conditions' which Offe sees as so intimately bound up with service work? Moreover, given the concerns of this book, we might also ask in what ways are sexual relations involved in the 'mediation' characteristic of service labour? Questions also flow from Urry's analysis of the organization of employment relations in tourism. For instance, just how significant are cultural relations, and especially the cultural expectations of consumers, in the formation of gendered work relations? In particular, do these cultural relations explain the concentration of women in 'front-line' occupations and the particular characteristics of work within the industry, such as employer interventions in the appearance and behaviour of these front-line workers? Finally, do sexual relations play a role in these dynamics? For example, are consumer expectations, and the characteristics of the industry such as the regulation of dress and behaviour, sexualized?

The study

To begin to explore the conditions of women's employment in tourist services, I undertook periods of fieldwork in two tourist establishments: a leisure park and a hotel. These focused on detailed observation and questioning around both the gendered structure of the organizations and the construction of work relations between men and women within employment situations. In particular, I was concerned to explore the significance of sexuality for the gendered organization of work relations.

Alongside this, I also investigated the gender and work relations of a particular occupation: hotel and catering establishment managers (notably pub and hotel managers). This latter part of the research concerned the relationship between family production and labour market work relations and involved interviews, observation and data collection not only from individual employees but also from the major employers within the industry.

The hotel and the leisure park in which the first strand of the fieldwork was based were very different from each other. The leisure park was located in a declining seaside resort in the north of England and was owned by a small local company. The park offered a number of facilities, including numerous 'fun rides', a children's amusement park, two licensed bars, catering outlets (including a restaurant and numerous food and drink kiosks situated around the park), souvenir shops, and a show-house where live performances were staged. All of these operations were located on the same site. The leisure park was relatively successful in relation to many other tourist and leisure facilities in the immediate locality, because it derived most of its custom from day-trippers from across the region rather than from holiday-makers. The presence of holiday-makers in the resort has been declining throughout the post-war period.

By contrast, the hotel was one of hundreds worldwide owned by a major international leisure company. The activities of this company, although spread broadly across leisure and tourism, centred on hotels and catering, and these accounted for over three-quarters of its turnover. The hotel itself, like the leisure park, was in the north of England, but it was located in a green-field site adjacent to a major motorway, close to a small city, rather than in a traditional tourist resort. The hotel's facilities included more than 100 bedrooms, a restaurant, a coffee bar, a licensed bar, a conference suite, a gym, sauna and swimming pool. Much of the hotel's custom derived directly from both the national and international conference trade, while other more casual custom came from motorway travellers and from visitors to a nearby national park. The restaurant, bar and health and fitness facilities also drew significant custom from the population of the local city.

Internally, both the hotel and the leisure park had a similar formal departmental structure (see Figs 1.1 and 1.2). At the leisure park there were five departments (marketing and sales, accounts, catering, the park department, and the bars department), while at the hotel there were six (sales and marketing, food and beverage, front of house, personnel and training, accounts, and health and fitness). At both the hotel and the leisure park, each of these departments had at least one manager, all of whom were responsible to the respective general managers of each establishment.

As well as having a similar internal structure, both the leisure park and the hotel made use of a variety of 'non-standard' workers. The leisure park, for example, had very few permanent workers (these included managers, secretaries and maintenance staff; see Table 1.1) and made extensive use of seasonal workers employed on temporary contracts from June to September of each year. (Indeed, the park was only fully open during this period. Outside of the summer months, only one bar was operated.) The temporary workers were employed in a variety of jobs, for example as ride operators, catering staff, shop workers, stage show personnel and bar staff. During the summer season, these workers constituted by far the majority of on-site employees. In 1989, for example, there were a total of 233 employees at the leisure park, of whom 217 (93 per cent) were seasonal workers, while the remaining 16 (7 per cent) were permanent staff (see Table 1.2).

In contrast to the leisure park, all the hotel's facilities were open all year round, but the hotel's workforce was nevertheless also divided into permanent and casual staff. The permanent staff included all of the managers and some receptionists, chefs and cooks, domestic staff, and porters and stewards (see Tables 1.3 and 1.4). During busy periods, for example during the summer months and times of peak conference trade, these permanent workers were augmented by casual workers employed on temporary contracts in a number of different capacities (e.g. bar staff, waiting staff and domestic staff). In the summer of 1989, of the 119 employees of Global Hotel, 61 (51 per cent) were permanent staff and 58 (49 per cent) were casual, temporary workers (see Table 1.4).

Many of the casual and seasonal employees, on whom both establishments relied heavily, were women. At the hotel, for example, 65 (55 per cent) of the 119 employees were women; of

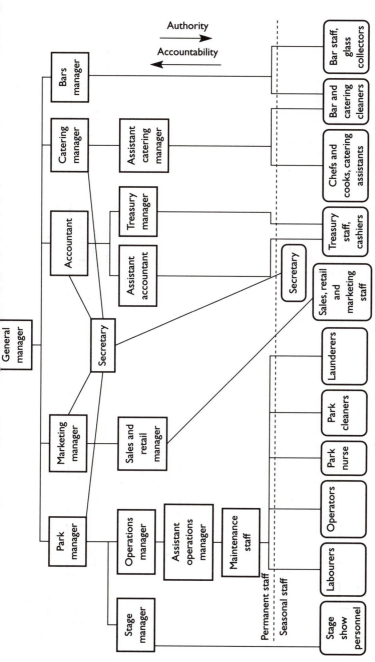

Figure 1.1 Internal organization of the leisure park: occupational hierarchy and lines of authority and accountability

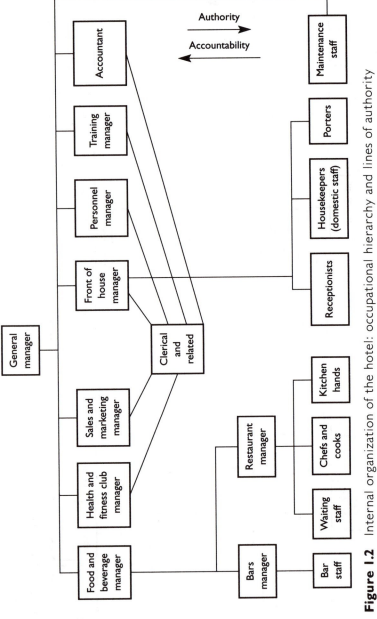

Figure 1.2 Internal organization of the hotel: occupational hierarchy and lines of authority and accountability

Table 1.1 Gender composition of permanent leisure park staff by occupation: summer 1989

Occupation	Men		Women		
	n	*%*	*n*	*%*	*Total*
Managers	10	77	3	23	13
Clerical and related	0	0	1	100	1
Maintenance staff	2	100	0	0	2
Total	12	75	4	25	16

Table 1.2 Gender composition of seasonal leisure park staff by occupation: summer 1989

Occupation	Men		Women		
	n	*%*	*n*	*%*	*Total*
Operatives	66	90	8	10	74
Catering assistants	18	35	33	65	51
Bar staff	10	45	12	55	22
Glass collectors	4	100	0	0	4
Retail and marketing	6	55	5	45	11
Treasury	6	100	0	0	6
Chefs and cooks	3	100	0	0	3
Launderers	0	0	1	100	1
Cleaners	14	56	11	44	25
Labourers	2	100	0	0	2
Cashiers	1	25	3	75	4
Nurses	0	0	1	100	1
Clerical and related	0	0	1	100	1
Dancers	4	40	6	60	10
Magicians	1	100	0	0	1
Sound and lighting operators	1	100	0	0	1
Total	136	62.5	81	37.5	217

these, 35 (54 per cent) were employed casually, whereas only 23 of the 54 (19 per cent) men were employed on this basis (see Tables 1.3 and 1.4). The leisure park employed a smaller, but still significant, proportion of women. Of the 233 employees, 148 (64 per cent) were men and 85 (36 per cent) women, but the majority of both men and women were employed as seasonal workers: 92 and 95 per cent, respectively (see Tables 1.1 and 1.2). Thus both the hotel

Table 1.3 Gender composition of all hotel staff (permanent and casual) by occupation: summer 1989

| | Men | | Women | | |
Occupation	n	%	n	%	Total
Managers	9	90	1	10	10
Clerical and related	0	0	4	100	4
Chefs and cooks	13	87	2	13	15
Kitchen hands	6	100	0	0	6
Receptionists	0	0	7	100	7
Bar staff	8	73	3	27	11
Waiting staff	9	29	22	71	31
Domestic staff	0	0	26	100	26
Porters	7	100	0	0	7
Maintenance staff	2	100	0	0	2
Total	54	45	65	55	119

and the leisure park were typical establishments within the tourist industry in their use of 'non-standard' labour and (especially in the case of the hotel) of women's temporary and casual labour. Furthermore, all of the employees – both men and women – at both the hotel and the leisure park were white.

The absence of black[2] workers and especially black women workers from both establishments was unusual, not least because the British tourist industry relies heavily on such employees, and because employed black women, especially Afro-Caribbean women, in Britain are clustered in just those manual service occupations typical of those in the hotel and leisure park (Brown 1984; Bryan *et al.* 1985; Phizacklea 1988a). However, this may be explained in part by the ethnic constitution of the area. The district in which both the hotel and the leisure park were located had an extremely small black population: 98.7 per cent of the population was white.[3] On the other hand, recent research on economic restructuring in Britain has suggested that formal employment opportunities are in fact becoming even more limited for black women (see Phizacklea 1988; Westwood and Bhachu 1988) and an important – but not often remarked – dimension of the growth in private consumer services industries,[4] and expanding areas of 'women's work' such as those contributing to Britain's tourist

Table 1.4 Gender composition of selected hotel occupations: summer 1989

Occupation	Men						Women						Total
	All		Permanent		Casual		All		Permanent		Casual		
	n	%	n	%	n	%	n	%	n	%	n	%	
Chefs and cooks	13	87	6	40	7	47	2	13	1	6.5	1	6.5	15
Kitchen hands	6	100	4	67	2	33	0	0	0	0	0	0	6
Bar staff	8	73	2	18	6	55	3	27	0	0	3	27	11
Waiting staff	9	29	3	10	6	19	22	71	3	10	19	61	31
Domestic staff	0	0	0	0	0	0	26	100	14	54	12	14	26
Porters	7	100	5	71	2	29	0	0	0	0	0	0	7
All others	11	48	11	48	0	0	12	52	12	52	0	0	23
Total	54	45	31	26	23	19	65	55	30	25.5	35	29.5	119

industry, is the general exclusion of black and migrant women from them (Phizacklea 1988a).

Thus, although there were important differences between the hotel and leisure park, in particular their different locations within 'leisure capital' and their different consumer profiles, many of their shared characteristics, especially the gender and 'race' profiles of their workforces and their employment practices, were representative of those of the tourist and consumer services in Britain generally. In addition, the patterns of segregation by gender within the occupations represented at the two establishments were also representative of the tourist industry as a whole.[5] At the leisure park, for instance, all of the maintenance staff were men, 77 per cent of managers, and 90 per cent of operatives (ride operators) were men, whereas women comprised 65 per cent of catering assistants and 75 per cent of cleaners. At the hotel, 90 per cent of managers and 87 per cent of chefs were men, whereas all of the receptionists and domestic staff were women (see Tables 1.1, 1.2 and 1.3).

Within these two fairly typical establishments, my investigation of the conditions of women's employment and the significance of sexuality in the organization and construction of work relations between men and women, found sexual work[6] relations to be central to both the gendered organization of work and the forms of control and exploitation to which women workers were subject. That is to say, the evidence showed sexual relations to be key to an understanding of the power relations between men and women in both workplaces. This constitutes not only a considerable challenge to the assumption within traditional labour market theory that sexuality is peripheral to employment and to the formation of work relations, but it also raises important questions in relation to more recent work which has sought actively to consider the relationship between sexuality and the gendered operations of the labour market. In particular, it questions the latter's understanding of the social structuring of sexuality and of the relationship between sexuality and employment work relations.

The second strand of my fieldwork, the study of the organization of gendered work relations in hotel and pub management, focused not on two specific locations but on a sample of employers and employees in relation to one occupation across the tourist industry. It looked at the relationship between family work relations and paid work relations within the labour market, and in particular at the significance of an employment practice used extensively throughout the hotel and catering sector of the tourist industry – that is, the employment of married couples to manage establishments (pubs and hotels). It was also concerned with the organization and construction of work relations between men and women, but in this case it focused on the relationship between husbands and wives and the forms of control and approbation of women's (wives') labour which operate in this particular occupation.

This made clear the relationship between family production (where goods and services are produced within family relations) and labour market work relations (where goods and services are produced within waged relations). As Chapter 3 will show, far from being outside the productive structure of the contemporary labour market, as is often assumed, family production in the case of hotel and catering establishment managers is actually located within the sphere of employment, and it directly structures gendered work relations. Hotel managers are almost always men, they are required to be married, and their wives' unpaid labour is used both by them as husbands and by their employers – even where the employers are multinational companies. Family production is therefore at the heart of the productive relations of this occupation. This challenges much in existing analyses of the gendered dynamics of the labour market, in particular assumptions about the forms of control and exploitation of women's labour power operating within the labour market, and about the nature of 'work' itself within the sphere of employment.

This last theme – the nature of labour market 'work' – is of particular significance to both the substantive areas of this book. Sexual employment relations and family production located within the wage-labour context are linked. They both show labour market 'work' and 'workers' to be gendered. However, as we shall see in Chapter 5, seeing and recognizing the labour market as so fundamentally gendered challenges many existing understandings of the gendered nature of employment relations and of the gendering of the contemporary labour market. This book is therefore of direct relevance to both labour market theory and theories of employment, and of special relevance to feminist labour market theory.

The argument established here is also important to analyses of the gender dynamics of sexuality, because it shows that sexuality intersects with work relations within the areas of employment under consideration, through structuring the gendered relations of production. This develops our understanding of the dynamics of gendered power relations and sexuality – of how sexuality comes to be structured by power relations between men and women, and hence advances the overall feminist project of understanding the tie between heterosexuality and gender in western societies.

Throughout this book the terms 'women workers' and 'men workers' are used to refer to women and men in employment and other work relations. While the use of the term 'women workers' is fairly widespread in studies of employment, that of 'men workers' is not. Men in employment relations are usually referred to as 'male workers', or sometimes just plain 'workers'. This practice is so common that the use of the term 'men workers' may, at times, appear rather awkward. However, the terms 'men workers' as well as 'women workers' have been consciously used in this book in order to recognize that both women workers *and* men workers constitute gendered social groups.

Notes

1 Belgium, Denmark, France, Germany, Ireland, Luxemburg, Netherlands, Spain and the UK.
2 The term 'black' is used here to refer to all the 'minority racial' groups in Britain, in particular Afro-Caribbean, African and South Asian.
3 Afro-Caribbeans comprised 0.06 per cent of the population, black Africans 0.07 per cent, Indians 0.04 per cent, Bangladeshis 0.01 per cent and Pakistanis 0.05 per cent.
4 Including hotels, guest houses, restaurants, cafes, pubs and clubs.
5 See Bagguley (1987) and Crompton and Sanderson (1990) for these general patterns.
6 The term 'sexual work' is used here to refer to work which involves a sexual element, such as responding to sexual innuendoes and wearing 'sexy' uniforms. It is, therefore, a broader term than – and is not synonymous with – 'sex-work', which is usually used to mean the commercial exchange of sex for money, such as in the case of prostitution.

2

Sexuality and the labour market

Throughout the 1970s and early 1980s, there was a proliferation of work on the labour market. Much of this work was a direct outcome of two major theoretical developments: dual or segmented labour market theory (see, for example, Doeringer and Piore 1971; Barron and Norris, 1976)[1] and Marxist labour process theory (most notably led by Braverman 1974). However, both were inadequate for the study of women's employment, in that they adopted a masculine conception of work and of workers, for example by focusing only upon manufacturing and thereby excluding the majority of employed women. The use of this kind of model meant that women's occupations and the position of women in employment were treated as deviant from a male norm.[2]

These kinds of problems with mainstream labour market theory led to considerable feminist critique (see, for example, the chapters in the Feminist Review collection, 1986), and to the development of specifically feminist analyses of the labour market. Much of this initial work came from Marxist feminists who attempted to reconstruct elements of Marxism and to provide a political economy of women's waged work. The most dominant strand in the UK took the form of fairly abstract accounts in which women were argued to constitute an industrial reserve army of labour for capital (see, e.g. Beechey 1978, 1982; Bruegel 1982, 1986). The lack of detailed empirical work to support these analyses led in turn to a general movement away from macro-theorizing about women's employment, to detailed ethnographies of workplaces and explorations of women's experiences of employment (see, e.g. Pollert 1981; Cavendish 1982; Wajcman 1983; Coyle 1984; Westwood 1984). However, much of this empirical work again focused upon manufacturing occupations, and therefore reproduced the bias of previous mainstream industrial sociology and labour market theory towards manual occupations, although some detailed studies of particular non-manual occupations did take place.[3]

Despite this movement away from general theorizing, during this period one of the most significant developments in feminist analyses of women's position in the labour market was published in the USA by Heidi Hartmann. Her two articles 'Capitalism, patriarchy, and job segregation by sex' (Hartmann 1979) and 'The unhappy marriage of Marxism and feminism: Towards a more progressive union' (Hartmann 1981) represented a radical break with past work on the nature of gendered divisions in the labour market. Hartmann stressed the role of autonomous patriarchal relations in the production of gendered inequalities within the labour market, in contrast to most previous (and indeed some current) theorists, who have concentrated exclusively upon the role of the relations and processes of capitalism (both inside and outside of the labour market).[4] More specifically, Hartmann suggested that with the development of capitalism, the labour market had become the major social site in which the material basis of patriarchy is secured, through men's control of women's labour. This control is maintained 'by excluding women from access to necessary economically productive resources' (Hartmann 1981:18), which in capitalist societies crucially includes exclusion from jobs that pay living wages (Hartmann 1981:15). It is men's control of women's access to places within the hierarchy of workers created by capitalism within the labour market which she claims forms the basis of men's control of women's labour (Hartmann 1981:18).

Hartmann provided extensive historical evidence to demonstrate the manner in which such control is manifest in the labour market. She pointed, for instance, to the role of men's labour organizations (in the form of guilds, fellowships, professions and trade unions) in limiting women's place in the labour market. These have often directly excluded women from access to occupations. She thus demonstrated the centrality of the actions of patriarchal agents for the production of the gender division of labour in the labour market, and in particular for the production of job segregation by sex. She claimed, indeed, that 'Job segregation by sex ... is the primary mechanism in capitalist society that maintains the superiority of men over women, because it enforces lower wages onto women in the labour market' (Hartmann 1979: 208).

Job segregation maintains the superiority of men over women because one of its major outcomes is the lowering of wages of women, which in turn keeps women dependent upon men.[5] Low wages encourage women to marry. This benefits men because within marriage women carry out unpaid domestic work for their husbands. Thus the control of women's labour in the labour market by men constituted the material basis of patriarchy. Hartmann suggested further that the central elements of patriarchy as currently experienced are:

> heterosexual marriage (and consequent homophobia), female child rearing and housework, women's economic dependence on men (enforced by arrangements in the labour market), the state, and numerous institutions based on social relations among men – clubs, sports, unions, professions, universities, churches, corporations, and armies.
>
> (Hartmann 1981: 19)

By focusing on the role of patriarchal agents in the labour market for the production of the gender division of labour, Hartmann's analysis broke away from many of the conventional modes of labour market analysis. Most importantly, it questioned the assumption that gender divisions and men's advantage over women in the labour market were an outcome of the relations of capitalism itself. The significance of this break cannot be underestimated. Until this point, many feminists had struggled to fit considerations of women's position in the labour market into an essentially unchanged Marxist analysis, often with unfortunate consequences. For example, attempts by Marxist feminists (e.g. Beechey 1978, 1982; Bruegel 1982) to argue that women formed a reserve army of labour for capital, that they were pulled into and pushed out of the labour market in line with the needs of capitalism, rested on biological assumptions about the formation of the gender division of labour outside the labour market – in the family.[6]

For instance, within reserve army theory itself, it was argued that it was women's role in the family which constituted them in their reserve army status. But this family role was taken for granted within the theory. In addition, the reserve army thesis was found wanting empirically: it could not explain the pattern of women's employment. It could not, for instance, explain the growth of women's employment in service industries and the simultaneous decline in men's employment in manufacturing industries during the 1980s.[7] What is more, by attempting to subsume inequalities of gender into the dynamics of capital, the reserve army thesis simply could not account for the actions of men in the labour market, such as those documented by Hartmann, for example, their organization to exclude women from particular occupations or from higher positions in a hierarchy. In assuming the gender division of labour in both the labour market and the family was an outcome of entirely capitalist processes, Marxist feminists naturalized gender divisions and, more particularly, ignored the significance of patriarchal agents in the formation of such divisions.

Since the publication of Hartmann's articles, the significnce of the actions of patriarchal agents for the production of the gender division of labour within the labour market has, however, been extensively documented (see, e.g. Braybon 1981; Cockburn 1983, 1985; Summerfield 1984; Walby 1986, 1990; Witz 1988). Walby (1986), for instance, has unravelled the significance of men's labour organizations (including trade unions), employers and the state (through protective legislation and unemployment policies) in producing the pattern of women's employment between 1800 and 1945 in Britain. Like Hartmann, Walby emphasizes the central significance of the control of women's access to wages in terms of explaining women's oppression within capitalism. She agrees with Hartmann that men's control over women's access to paid work acts as a key mechanism through which women's dependency upon men is maintained, and it is through this that the conditions which allow men to exploit women's domestic labour in the family are provided. Indeed, Walby (1986: 55) suggests that 'patriarchal relations in paid work are necessary, if not sufficient, to the retention of women as unpaid labourers in the household', because by limiting women's access to paid work, men maintain a situation where women have little choice but to marry. In so doing, men secure access to women's unpaid domestic production in the household. Unlike Hartmann, Walby drew extensively on the work of Christine Delphy (1970, 1984) to argue that within the household or family a distinct mode of production – the patriarchal mode of production – is in operation.

Delphy argues that when production occurs in the context of the family, women work within a relationship to effect that production which is comparable to serfdom. Housework, for example, is done free by women in the context of the family, that is without remuneration. The beneficiaries of this labour – heads of households, that is, usually husbands – maintain the labour of their wives in 'exchange' for domestic labour. This is an obligation placed on men, but one which, Delphy points out, is clearly in their own interests. Family production is therefore characterized by the appropriation and exploitation of women's (and sometimes other household members', such as children's) labour by adult men/ husbands.

These sets of relations exist whenever the unit of production is the family, including when goods and services are produced which are intended for sale on the market. Delphy points, for example, to the case of small family farms in France, where as well as carrying out unpaid domestic production, wives (and until the late 1960s unmarried brothers and sisters, and sons and daughters) of farmers carry out substantial amounts of non-remunerated agricultural work. The structuring of the relations of the family means that whatever goods are produced in this context belong to the household head, that is, dependants' and wives' labour is appropriated and exploitated. Wives' and dependants' production has no exchange value when they work within the framework of the family. Wives themselves do not make use of their labour; husbands do. Where husbands use their wives' labour in the family production of goods and services which are sold on the market, it is husbands alone who exchange the products on the market. In the same way, Delphy argues, a woman does not make use of her domestic work when it is performed within the family, not because wives' production has no value, but rather because wives' family production is excluded from the market. The specificity of the relationship of wives to family production means that these relations of production constitute a distinct mode of production – the patriarchal mode of production (which is separate from the capitalist mode of production). In the patriarchal mode of production, there are two classes: wives (the producing class) and husbands (the appropriating class).

Walby drew on this analysis when constructing her theory of women's oppression, but unlike Delphy she argues that women's position within domestic production is a direct outcome of men's control of women's access to wages within the labour market: 'the primary mechanism which ensures that women will serve their husbands is their exclusion from paid work on the same terms as men' (Walby 1986: 54). For both Hartmann and Walby, then, within the context of capitalism it is men's control of women's labour in the labour market (in the form of control to access to wages) that forms the key mechanism through which men maintain material power over women.

The control of women's access to wage-labour and gender

Both Walby and Hartmann also point in their analyses to the existence of other areas of inequality between men and women. But they present these as external to the control and exploitation of women's labour. Hartmann, for instance, as already seen, argues that current elements of patriarchy include heterosexual marriage and consequent homophobia, and institutions based on social relations between men; while Walby recognizes that inequality exists between men and women in terms of sexuality and violence. However, their systematic foregrounding of men's control of women's access to waged labour as *the* material basis of patriarchy within the context of capitalism makes it difficult to see any exact connections between the control of access to wages and these other forms of inequality. If, as they suggest, control of access to wages forms the key to relations between men and women, then presumably these 'other' inequalities are an outcome of women's disadvantaged labour market position. But the problem is that neither Hartmann nor Walby actually demonstrates how the control of women's access to waged labour leads to, or provides the conditions for, other inequalities to be produced (other than in relation to domestic labour).

As regards sexuality, while they go further than many other theorists who have paid attention to the formation of gender divisions within the labour market, in that they acknowledge the existence of inequality between men and women in the sexual domain (in particular, they go further than many Marxist feminists who up to this point had largely ignored sexuality), it is nevertheless at the periphery of their respective analyses. When sexuality is mentioned by either Hartmann or Walby, they imply either that control of access to wages somehow causes inequalities in relation to sexuality outside the labour market, or they simply leave unclear how such inequalities come into being. (It could be that it is because of the compulsion to marry that women have to enter into heterosexual social relations, but Hartmann and Walby never spell out such a sequence.)

This confusion is well exemplified in Hartmann's (1981: 15) assertion that 'men maintain this control [over women's labour] by excluding women from access to some essential productive resources ... and by restricting women's sexuality'. The precise meaning of this statement is unclear. It implies that the restriction of women's sexuality, in addition to the control of women's access to wages, somehow constitutes a dimension of the control of women's labour, but Hartmann does not specify how this restriction has such an effect. Indeed, 'sexuality' floats into, and out of, Hartmann's (1981) analysis in a rather *ad hoc* manner, and at no time does she really tackle the relationship between the control of women's labour and inequalities in relation to sexuality.

What is clear in both of these analyses, however, despite these ambiguities, is that neither Hartmann nor Walby consider the relations of sexuality to have a bearing upon the formation of the gender division of labour within the labour market itself. Indeed, both analyses suggest that they do not consider 'sexuality' to operate within the labour market at all. Walby (1986: 247), for instance, locates sexuality as existing in civil society, that is somewhere 'outside' of the economy and also of the state; while Hartmann tends to associate the operation of sexuality with the family, particularly with monogomous marriage, which she certainly also separates from the labour market.

The location of sexuality as exogenous to the labour market derives from the assumptions that sexuality is a 'non-economic' phenomenon, and that the labour market is an entity whose structure is primarily determined by economic relations. In both

Hartmann's and Walby's accounts, while patriarchal relations are seen to operate to determine who fills what places within the hierarchy of waged workers (albeit there are struggles around this, see especially Walby's account), the formation of this hierarchy itself (that is, the creation of places within a hierarchy of waged workers) is seen as a product of the relations of capitalism. Thus, the labour market is an arena which they define as being constituted by ungendered economic relations, or 'capital' as it has been conventionally defined (Adkins and Lury 1992). For both Walby and Hartmann, men's material power over women is constituted in terms of their greater access to the (ungendered) economic resources created by capital. And this definition of both the labour market and men's material power over women in terms of (ungendered) economic relations leads both authors to locate sexuality as exogenous to the labour market. Sexuality is differentiated from both men's material power and the labour market, in that the 'sexual' is seen to take a non-economic form. While both authors recognize sexuality as an area in which inequality exists between men and women, they define it as existing outside of capital–labour relations, and hence as exogenous to the labour market, and as thoroughly peripheral to the main arena of control of women's labour.

Given the overall significance that Walby and Hartmann accord the control of women's access to waged labour in terms of women's general subordination to men, it follows that for them this control must be central to the formation of gender, that is the social production of men and women. This is clearly stated by Hartmann:

> ... gender production grows out of the extant division of labour between the sexes ... In my view, because of these deep ramifications of the sexual division of labor we will not eradicate sex-ordered task division until we eradicate the socially imposed gender differences between us and, therefore, the very sexual division of labor itself.
>
> (Hartmann 1979: 231–2)

In other words, gender is produced by the sexual division of labour, and given that the sexual division of labour to which Hartmann is referring is that within the labour market (which is in turn produced by men's control of women's access to paid work), gender is therefore seen by Hartmann to be produced by men's control of women's employment possibilities. While this position is not explicated by Walby, it is nevertheless a conclusion which can be fairly safely drawn about her work too. Her analysis, like Hartmann's, centres on the control of women's access to wages, and then on the consequences of occupational segregation by sex for women's general position in relation to men. It must be job segregation by sex which explains, *inter alia*, the domestic mode of production.

Thus while Walby and Hartmann do pay some attention to sexuality, they accord it little if any significance as a gendered form of control operating within the labour market. Nor do they see sexuality as important in the production of occupational segregation, nor indeed in the creation of gender itself. Indeed, since Walby's and Hartmann's analyses recognize that inequalities with respect to sexuality exist, and since they also simultaneously argue that men's control of women's access to wages constitutes the material basis of patriarchy, the fact that they do not provide an explanation of the ways in which such control leads to such inequality constitutes a theoretical void in their work. Put like this, it seems that Walby and Hartmann would both conclude that inequalities between men and women in relation to sexuality must somehow be an outcome of men's control of women's access to wages, rather than being in any way independently constitutive of women's oppression.

Even in Walby's (1990) later work, where she argues that sexuality, or more particularly heterosexuality, forms a distinct set of patriarchal relations, she nevertheless asserts that the dominant sets of patriarchal relations – those which are most significant in terms of the production of gender – are patriarchal relations in employment. And she again states that it is the control of women's access to wages (most particularly in the form of practices which segregate women into low-grade jobs) and patriarchal relations in the state which are key. So while she has gone some way towards recognizing that sexuality constitutes a specific set of relations, these relations remain peripheral to, and unexplicated by, her overall scheme. Unlike her earlier work, Walby's recent analysis does suggests that sexuality operates within the labour market, but only inasmuch as it may contribute to the control of women's access to jobs and wages (Walby 1990: 39).

Heterosexuality and the control and exploitation of women's labour

The minimal significance attached to sexuality in the construction of women's oppression by Hartmann and Walby is in complete opposition to many other feminist analyses. Radical feminists, in particular, have contended that 'sexuality' constitutes a set of social relations through which gender inequality is produced (rather than being an outcome of some other sets of relations). And some radical feminists have even argued that it is primarily or even exclusively through sexuality, and *because of* sexuality, that men are able, and seek, to control women. Indeed, some argue that sexuality constitutes gender (e.g. MacKinnon 1987, 1989). Moreover, these radical feminist accounts of sexuality constitute one of the few approaches to sexuality which highlights any kind of connection between the gendered structuring of sexuality *and* the control and approbation of women's labour, including the exploitation of women's labour in employment.

While sexuality in everyday accounts is often viewed as largely natural behaviour, almost all researchers in the field see it as either substantially, or almost entirely, socially structured.[8] Relatively few of these analysts, however, recognize the central significance of gender in this social structuring of sexuality, and still fewer question or problematize 'normal' sexuality, that is heterosexuality. That is to say, few recognize the significance of sexuality in the production of wider gender inequality and its central contribution to the production of gender itself. Radical feminist analyses of sexuality, however, can perhaps be characterized by, and distinguished from, other analyses of sexuality by the very fact of their insistence on the centrality of the unequal structuring of sexual relations between men and women, and their emphasis on questioning and explaining this structuring.

These starting points have been found by some to be controversial, and have often lead to an outright rejection of such analyses or a sidestepping of rather than an engagement with them (e.g. Vance 1984; Segal 1987; Segal and McIntosh 1992). A whole body of feminist and non-feminist empirical research substantiates the central claims of radical feminist analyses, however. For example, a range of research on everyday socially acceptable sexual interactions between men and women has shown the ways in which sexuality is dominated by men, and how women almost never exchange sex for sex. Rather they engage in different kinds of sexual–economic exchange, lying 'along a continuum from marriage to occasional or long lasting relations with friends, "paying fiances" . . . and regular clients' (Tabet 1989: 206 – see also Tabet 1987).

It has been confirmed, for instance, that men are the ones who take action/initiatives and have the 'right' to define and control sexual situations;[9] that a sexual double standard exists for men and women and that restrictive dichotomies operate which define women as either madonnas or whores/sexual drags or slags (Lees 1986, 1993; Bland 1988); and that men control and define actual sexual practice, for example by defining heterosexual sex as over when they themselves have reached orgasm (Lyndon 1970; Koedt 1970; Whiting 1972; Rubin 1979). It has also been revealed that men use a vocabulary of sexual abuse directed towards women on an everyday basis (see, e.g. Wood 1984; Mahoney 1985; Laws 1990) and the ambivalence women feel with regard to sexual relations with men (Oakley 1981).

Research has also shown the extent to which women are coerced sexually. A random sample of women in San Francisco found that 44 per cent of women said they had been victims of rape or attempted rape at least once in their lives (Russell 1982; Russell and Howell 1983), and 38 per cent of girls and 10 per cent of boys reported being sexually abused as children (Russell 1984). A study of the federal workplace in the USA found that 42 per cent of all women employees reported being sexually harassed (US Merit Systems Protection Board 1981, cited by Hadjifotiou 1983: 8), while other studies have shown the incidence of sexual harassment to be even higher, ranging between 60 and 96 per cent (Alfred Marks Bureau 1982; Leeds TUCRIC 1983. On the basis of her various studies of sexual violence, Diana Russell has estimated that only 7.8 per cent of American women have not been sexually assaulted or harassed in their lifetime (cited in MacKinnon 1987: 6). Other studies have shown that diverse forms of men's sexual violence, including the threat of violence, pressurized and coercive sex, flashing, obscene 'phone calls, and sexual assault, are daily occurrences in women's lives (see Russell 1982, 1984; Bart and O'Brien 1985; Stanko 1985, 1990; Hanmer and Maynard 1987; Kelly 1988; Hanmer et al. 1989). Or again, that women are compelled into a form of sexual practice which puts them at maximum risk of pregnancy and infection, while their access to contraception and abortion is restricted (Tabet 1985; Holland *et al.* 1990). These events are both controlling and help significantly to shape social life for women.

That sexual violence and forms of sexual exploitation are a pervasive feature of women's lives (Barry 1979; Russell 1984), that 'acceptable' sexuality is structured by power imbalances between men and women, and that intimate relationships between women are defined as deviant, suggests that sexuality is organized in a way in which male dominance becomes 'normal'. This link is central for understanding the social organization of sexuality (Jackson 1978; MacKinnon 1987, 1989; Kelly 1988), and it leads radical feminists directly to a problematization of heterosexuality. Thus Adrienne Rich (1983), for example, argues that pervasive forms of sexual violence against women are linked to one central process – the enforcement of heterosexuality on women. She links direct force (including sexual violence, forms of sexual slavery and heterosexual pressures on women) with what she refers to as 'subliminal enforcement' (or the control of consciousness), through the idealization of heterosexual romance and marriage (which asserts that women are inevitably, even if 'rashly and tragically', drawn to men); the erasure of lesbian existence; and the mass dissemination of pornography in which women are represented as commodities for men's consumption. All make heterosexuality 'compulsory' for women. Far from being a voluntary choice or preference, heterosexuality is 'imposed, managed, organized, propagandized and maintained by force' (Rich 1983: 191). She argues that heterosexuality needs therefore to be examined as a political institution, and she says failure to do so is 'like failing to admit that the economic system called capitalism or the caste system of racism is maintained by a variety of forces' (Rich 1983: 192).

For Rich, these processes of enforcement, and the consequent production of compulsory heterosexuality, act 'as a means of assuring male right of physical, economical, and emotional access' (Rich 1983: 191). Male-dominated sexuality, as part of the process of enforcement of compulsory heterosexuality, is seen not simply in terms of a mechanism through which women are controlled in the arena of the conventionally sexual – that is, in the arena of heterosexual sexual practices – but as a mechanism through which all manner of forms of domination are produced. Rich includes here the power of men to command or exploit women's labour and to control their produce (through, for example, the institutions of marriage and motherhood as unpaid production, and the horizontal segregation of women in paid employment); to control or rob women of their children (through, for example, father-right and 'legal kidnapping'); to confine women physically and prevent movement (through rape as terrorism, 'feminine' dress codes, the enforced economic dependence of wives); and to use women in male transactions (through bride-price, arranged marriages, and the use of women as entertainers to facilitate men's deals, e.g. wife-hostesses, geishas, escorts and secretaries).

'Compulsory heterosexuality' thus not only means men's sexuality is forced onto women, that is to say it not only produces exploitation and inequality in sexual practices, but also, according to Rich, it is connected to, indeed produces – all manner of forms of gender inequality. She suggests that heterosexuality, far from being simply a sexual practice, is a system of social relations which maintains men's power over women. For her, sexuality has central significance in the formation of gender (the social production of men and women). Rich's analysis of compulsory heterosexuality as both social and political, placed what had often been previously seen as 'natural', as social and key to the construction and perpetuation of gender inequalities. She drew connections between male-dominated sexuality and 'other' forms of gender inequality, such as those in employment and in marriage, and in so doing placed a consideration of the social relations of sexuality firmly on the agenda for an understanding of women's oppression.

Other radical feminists have also seen the social construction of heterosexuality as central to understanding gender inequalities. Raymond (1986), for instance, argues that hetero-relations, which give men constant access to women – economically, socially, politically, affectively and sexually – give rise to what she refers to as 'hetero-reality'. Hetero-reality, she says, refers to an ontology within which women always and only exist in relation to men, and all social relations are constituted through this principle: 'we live in a hetero-relational society where most of women's personal, social political, professional and economic relations are defined by the ideology that woman is for man' (Raymond 1986: 11). For Raymond, hetero-reality means: 'All life becomes a metaphor for marriage. Every social relation demands its other half, its cosmic complement. The two must become one, whether in the bedroom or board room' (ibid.: 12). In other words, all social relations, by operating through the principles of hetero-reality, ensure men's access to women because women are always defined in relation to men – to exist for the use of, and to complement, men.

What is clearly of significance in such analyses is that they posit heterosexuality as the set of relations through which men control and exploit women's labour (among other things). Rich, for instance, suggests that through compulsory heterosexuality women's labour is controlled, both inside and outside the labour market. Similarly, Raymond argues that through hetero-reality men gain direct access to, and can appropriate, the products of women's economic/productive activities. This is clearly in marked contrast to the analyses of the labour market discussed earlier, which attribute sexuality little if any significance in terms of the control and exploitation of women's labour.

Some radical feminists indeed argue that gender is completely constituted or determined by sexuality. For example MacKinnon (1987: 49) argues '. . . the moulding, direction, and expression of sexuality organizes society into two sexes, women and men. This division underlies the totality of social relations'. Unlike Rich, however, for MacKinnon it is not just that heterosexuality is a system of social relations through which a range of power relations between men and women are constituted, but rather that social relations themselves (and therefore the whole gender system) are sexualized. To put it rather simply, while Rich expands the sexual by linking it to the social, MacKinnon argues that the social itself is intrinsically sexual.

MacKinnon believes the sexualization of social relations, and the creation of gender, occurs through the eroticization of the relations of dominance and subordination: 'male and female are created through the eroticization of dominance and submission' (MacKinnon 1983: 635). The central social process or dynamic of the eroticization of dominance and submission, and the creation of sexualized inequality, she claims is sexual objectification (MacKinnon 1982: 253), that is the reduction of women to sexual objects, or things to be used:

...women's sexual desirability is fetishized: it is made to appear a quality of the object itself, spontaneous and inherent, independent of the social relation that creates it, uncontrolled by the force that requires it.

(MacKinnon 1989: 123)

This argument has, however, proved to be controversial. For example, a problem which is often cited in relation to her analysis is that in arguing sexuality creates gender, MacKinnon places too much weight on the significance of sexuality for the production of forms of gender inequality. Valverde (1989), for instance, argues that MacKinnon over-emphasizes the sexual component of women's oppression to the detriment of economic and social factors which are of significance in terms of the production of gender inequality. Similarly, Walby (1990: 119) argues that MacKinnon's analysis of the formation of gender dismisses the significance of forms of men's power which 'are not articulated through sexuality in an *a priori* fashion'. But as has been suggested by Raymond and Rich, 'economic' and 'social' factors, and other forms of men's power over women, are all arguably 'sexual', in that they may be connected to heterosexuality.

But a major problem with these analyses is that when they argue that sexuality forms the totality of gender, they do not explicate what the connections are between heterosexuality and all forms of gender inequality. Thus Rich and Raymond themselves do not explain or attempt to uncover actual connections between sexuality and the control of women's labour. It is not at all clear how the compulsion on women to be heterosexual leads to, or provides the conditions through which, their labour gets controlled and used by men. Rather, the posited connection is simply part and parcel of the placing of heterosexuality and the appropriation of sexual servicing as the main thing men get from women, as central to the formation of all forms of gender inequality. So one of the major questions which clearly emerges from the above discussion has to be to what extent (if at all) can forms of control and the exploitation of women's labour be seen to be connected to heterosexuality? In addition, in the light of MacKinnon's analysis, it also needs to be asked whether or not such appropriation may be sexualized.

Broadening out gender in the labour market: critiques of the 'economic'

So far in this chapter the only feminist analyses of the labour market which have been discussed have been those which view the control of women's access to wages as key to understanding the production of men's advantage and women's subordination. Other feminists have, however, been critical of these approaches and argue that there are other dimensions of patriarchal power in the labour market. In her early work, Cynthia Cockburn (1981, 1983, 1985), for example, argued that men exert not just economic power but also what she referred to as socio-political power and physical power over women. By socio-political she meant men's organization and solidarity and the significance of such institutions as unions, clubs and societies in the construction of men's material power; while physical power referred to men's physical advantages over women, including bodily strength and capability and their control over machinery and tools (Cockburn 1981: 43).

Within this analysis, Cockburn's attention to the 'physical' was particularly unusual, for, as she noted, many feminists had avoided considering this form of power because of assumed essentialist connotations. She maintained, however, that men's physical advantage over women, and the power it confers, is socially constructed and politically organized. She argued that physical efficiency and technical capability do not belong to men by birth, but rather are appropriated by men throughout their lifetime (Cockburn 1981: 43). Cockburn saw men's socio-political and economic power as providing the conditions through which this appropriation could take place, and 'in turn, their physical presence reinforces their authority and their physical skills enhance their earning power' (ibid.).

Cockburn (1981: 44) identified a range of social practices as constitutive of men's relative bodily advantage over women, including 'the accumulation of bodily capacities, the definition of tasks to match them and the selective design of tools and machines', and she showed their implications for the gendering of the labour market. They mean, for instance, that women are often excluded from manual occupations and from the control of technology. In relation to the occupation of printing compositors, for instance, Cockburn (1983: 203) argued that it is 'one of the many "male jobs" that has contributed to the construction of men as strong, manually able and technologically endowed, and women as physically and technically incompetent'. In printing, men have appropriated the physical and mental properties and technical hardware required for compositing. This has meant that it has remained the preserve of men. Cockburn revealed how these processes operated through consecutive rounds of technological restructuring within the compositing labour process. For instance, an attempt by employers to introduce women to typesetting following its mechanization in the early 1900s was thwarted by organized compositors, who were able to achieve this because 'their socio-political power enabled them to extend their physical capabilities in manual typesetting to control of the machine that replaced it' (Cockburn 1981: 47).

Thus, men have been able to turn their bodily advantage over women into economic and social advantage within the labour market through the process of the manipulation of physical and technical differences between men and women. They have defined into occupations the requirements of physical strength and technical competence with which (only) they are socially endowed:

> ... men have built their own relative bodily and technical strength by depriving women of theirs, and they have organized their occupation in such a way as to benefit from the differences they have constructed. The attributes of strength and skill have also been deployed competitively in the manoeuvring for status between men in the male hierarchy that dominates women.
>
> (Cockburn 1983: 204)

Through her broadening out of the material dimensions of men's power, Cockburn revealed how the construction of the gender division of labour in the labour market was not simply an 'economic' matter, but also involved the manipulation of (socially constituted) bodily capabilities. In so doing, she challenged what was becoming something of an orthodoxy in feminist labour market theory, namely the assumption that the material dimensions of women's oppression were synonymous with economic relations (for example, the production of men's greater earning power).

Cockburn located this assumption as particularly evident in Marxist feminist accounts of women's position in the labour market, especially those accounts which argued that capital uses women's labour as an industrial reserve army of labour. She argued that this formulation was limited because it obscured other important material practices constitutive of women's oppression. Indeed, she argued 'that it is only by thinking with the additional concepts of the socio-political and the physical that we can begin to look for material instances of male domination beyond men's greater earning power and property advantage' (Cockburn 1981: 43).[10]

But despite the significance of Cockburn's identification of the problems associated with narrow economic analyses, and the importance of her reformulations of the material aspects of men's power over women and the construction of the gender division of labour in the labour market, her analysis, nevertheless, does suffer from some of the same problems as the economistic accounts. In particular, like Hartmann and Walby, her analysis pays little attention to sexuality, and even when sexuality is mentioned it is treated rather ambiguously. At one point, for instance, she suggests that the physical dimension of men's material power also includes sexual dominance: 'a special degree of importance adheres to the physical and the social, to sexuality for instance' (Cockburn 1983: 196). But while this certainly implies seeing sexuality as an important element of men's material power, Cockburn did not explicate how, nor in what ways, the sexual forms part of this power, despite the fact that in her empirical studies she does record a range of sexual practices operating within the labour market. For example, in her study of printers, she noted how the workplace walls 'were unashamedly covered with pin-ups' (Cockburn 1983: 186) and how men wanted 'women's sexuality as free currency. This is the meaning ascribed to women in the compositor's workplace culture' (ibid.: 185). Similarly, in her study of techno-logical change in three industries, she records how 'men relate through competitive swearing, obscenity and a trade in sexual stories, references and innuendo that are directly objectifying and exploitative of women' (Cockburn 1985: 176). But she did not tackle the issue of how these kinds of sexualized practices contributed to the formation of men's material advantage in the labour market. Most notably, she did not attempt to link them to the processes of occupational structuring and the formation of the gender division of labour (as she had, for example, in relation to control over machinery and tools). Thus the issue of how, or in what ways, the day-to-day sexual objectification of women by men compositors related to the power of this group of workers to organize their occupation, and exclude women from it, was not tackled.

This separation of sexuality from the processes of gendered structuring of the labour market, and lack of consideration of their relationship, is not specific to Cockburn's work, however. It is a characteristic common to many analyses which explicitly set out to give attention to 'non-economic' processes in the gendering of the labour market. For example, in her historical study of gendered job segregation, Bradley (1989) argues, like Cockburn, that focusing on the economic aspects of women's oppression in the labour market (in particular, the control of women's labour) ignores other important elements of men's power over women. Indeed, she specifically suggests that it obscures 'other aspects of the relations between men and women that go on in the family and elsewhere: the dominant role of men in sexuality for example' (Bradley 1989: 54). But despite this recognition of the sexual inequalities of men and women, and the documentation of sexuality operating in the labour market,[11] Bradley, like Cockburn, does not pay attention to the relationship between sexuality and the processes of gender segregation. It is thus not at all clear, for example, if in her analysis men's sexual domination contributes to the process of gender segregation, or if it is an outcome of segregation itself. Sexuality is left freestanding, as an unexplicated phenomenon.

It is ironic that analyses which have attempted to move away from the problems associated with economistic frameworks should have reproduced many of the same difficulties. In particular, that the status of some of the 'non-economic' processes has remained the same in both types of accounts, as in the case of sexuality.

Gendered workers and the specifity of women's labour

Despite the constant peripheralization of sexuality in most feminist analyses of the labour market, there have nevertheless been some very important recent theoretical developments in this field. In particular, attention has turned to thinking about the specificity of women's labour, especially the ways in which the exploitation of women's labour differs from that of men's in the labour market. For example, in her recent work Cockburn (1991; following Mies 1986) has argued that women are not 'free' wage earners in the same way as men, in that prior demands are made on their labour, especially in the family, which mean that women are not as free to exchange their labour as men. These prior demands on women's labour are seen to mean that women do not own their labour in the same way as men and, in turn, that women's labour is particularly exploitable in the labour market: women are unable to sell their labour at the same rate as men. Mies and Cockburn both suggest that the 'domestically defined female sex' rather than the 'free proletarian' is currently the optimal labour force for capital. Recent economic restructuring, for example, including the decline in manufacturing, the increasing use of subcontracting, the growth of services and the increasing casualization of employment, has been predicated on the use of women's labour rather than men's, as witnessed in the use of women's labour in part-time work, homeworking, the new service industries and in export processing zones. At the same time, however, families are increasingly dependent on women's (inadequate) wages and upon their continued, and in many cases increasing, domestic and caring workload (Morris 1990; Glendinning and Millar 1992).

Cockburn suggests this exploitation of women's work in the labour market does not fall on women accidentally; far from it, 'it is sex-specific and in fact is constructed within the terms of . . . her subordination to husband, her responsibility for child, other dependants and home' (Cockburn 1991: 84). Thus Cockburn, like Mies, suggests that the exploitation of women's labour in the labour market does not take place under the same terms as that of men, and that the 'narrow capitalist (and Marxist) concept of productive labour – the paradigm case of which is the male proletarian – has to be recast' (ibid.). Cockburn argues that such a recasting requires bringing into view the hidden non-wage labour of women 'as subsistence farmers, as producers of under-priced commodities, and as unpaid housewives' (ibid.).

Importantly, Cockburn maintains that this sex-specific exploitation of women's labour does not only operate for married women, but is also at play for women who are not married.

Cockburn argues the latter are always assumed to be dependants and obliged to sell their labour at a reduced rate. Perhaps more importantly, however, as Delphy and Leonard (1992) have shown, women who are not married are also subject to the appropriation of their labour by men family members other than their husbands. Thus, after divorce, the labour of ex-wives often continues to be appropriated by ex-husbands for child-care, and brothers are regularly exonerated from huge amounts of work via sisters' care of elderly parents.

Delphy and Leonard's analysis of the gendered and generational structuring of the family parallels that of Mies in stressing that the particular forms of exploitation of women's work in the family mean that they cannot sell their labour on the same terms as men. Family subordinates – in which they include wives and children and especially daughters – do not own their labour power in the same way as heads of households, because their work is appropriated through the structuring of marital and familial relations. Marriage, for example, gives husbands rights to the unlimited use of wives' work, and wives' familial duties involve an obligation to devote whatever of their time and energy is needed to provide whatever their husbands require (Delphy and Leonard 1992: 118). This analysis, and in particular their central notion that family subordinates do not own their labour power, means that wives and daughters are 'not free to sell their labour to a third party without their household head authorizing it ... and if they [do] sell it to someone else, they do so under limiting conditions' (Delphy and Leonard 1992: 119).

A number of studies have revealed the existence of limiting conditions operating in relation to wives' and daughters' (and other women family members') employment, but not operating for husbands/men. For example, wives' employment is conditional on their husbands' approval (Martin and Roberts 1984). Some wives have been found to keep their jobs secret from their husbands, in the knowledge that if they found out, they would not allow them to remain in employment, or register extreme discontent and make the women's lives extremely difficult (Porter 1983; Martin and Roberts 1984). But while husbands exert control over whether or not their wives have jobs, and what type of jobs they do have, they make their own decisions about their own jobs with little or no consultation with their wives, and with little or no consideration for the effects of their hours and the location of the job on the rest of the household (Porter 1983).

A number of studies have confirmed wives are still defined as housekeepers and mothers first, and wage workers second, whereas the opposite has been found for men (Porter 1983; Martin and Roberts 1984). Finch (1983) lists a set of priorities within marriage for wives: the husband and his requirements, including those of his job, take priority; then come the requirements of children; and third – and only when husbands' and children's requirements are met – may wives' needs be considered. This places servere limitations not only on their employment possibilities, but also finds expression in a whole series of calculations which are made regarding whether or not it is 'worth' their seeking employment . Thus travel expenses, the cost of childcare, clothing and other expenses, and extra taxes which may be incurred, are added up and subtracted from the women's earnings to establish whether they *should* seek employment or not. The same calculations are not made *vis-à-vis* men's work. Rather, the costs incurred by the husband's employment are seen as legitimate *household* expenses from *joint* money. Once in employment, further limitations operate for wives. First, they still have to do the bulk of the domestic work – and all the other forms of work required by the head of household (childcare, for example, or help with *his* profession) – and this work takes precedence not only over their waged work but also their leisure and their sleep (Meissner *et al.* 1988).

There are also numerous family-related restrictions operating for women who are not wives. Grown-up daughters, for example, may have their employment possibilities constrained through caring for parents, especially widowed fathers and elderly mothers (Leonard 1980). Younger daughters may be restricted in their education or vocational training, as well as in their employment possibilities, because they are required to care for younger siblings, grandparents or other relatives, or to do domestic work (Shaw 1981; Griffin 1985). In addition, childcare, elder and sick care, and the maintenance of kin contact between households, is regularly carried out by less clearly related women family members – by aunts, sisters, sisters-in-law and grandmothers (Finch and Groves 1983; Leonardo 1987; Finch 1989).

There is thus a very extensive body of research documenting the various ways women are not free to exchange their labour with employers on the same terms as men due to the non-ownership and appropriation of their labour in the family, and the fact that as women they can never have the back-up provided by a wife. This situation is summed up by Pateman (1988: 131):

> ... women cannot become 'workers' in the same sense as men
> ... the employment contract presupposes the marriage
> contract ... the construction of the 'worker' presupposes that
> he is a man who has a woman, a (house)wife to take care of his
> daily needs.

Thus for Pateman the ability to 'freely' contract with an employer – to sell labour power – is a distinctly gendered phenomenon. Only men are free 'workers' and the ability to be a 'worker' is founded upon men's control and use of women's labour in marriage. Pateman maintains that it is this – that women do not constitute 'workers' in the same way as men, that they are not free workers – which explains why women are not incorporated into workplaces on the same basis as men workers, why 'most women can find paid employment only in a narrow range of low-status, low-paid occupations, where they work alongside other women and are managed by men' (Pateman 1988: 132).

The idea found in Pateman's, Delphy and Leonard's, Cockburn's and Mies' analyses – that what constitutes a 'worker' is a gendered phenomenon – together with the body of research which supports this contention, provides a considerable challenge to some of the earlier analyses of the labour market discussed in this chapter, especially those which separate out capitalist and patriarchal social relations. In Hartmann and Walby's analyses, for example, capitalism and patriarchy are held as distinct, yet interrelating – sets of social relations. That is to say, the labour market is defined as an entity constructed through the relations of capitalism, on top of which patriarchal relations get played out and reconstituted. But the analyses of Pateman *et al.* suggest that far from being a separate phenomenon, capitalism itself is patriarchal. In this view, the labour market, rather than being just a capitalist construct, is equally a patriarchal one. Thus, for example, the 'worker' is not simply created through capitalist relations, but depends for his existence on patriarchal relations. As Pateman (1988: 135) put it: 'the attributes and activities of the "worker" are constructed together with, and as the other side of, those of his feminine counterpart, the (house)wife'. Indeed, Acker (1989) has explicitly critiqued the 'dual systems' approach for differentiating between different systems or regimes of social relations. In particular, she suggests that such approaches 'leave intact the patriarchal assumptions buried in theories about the other systems to which patriarchy is related' (Acker 1989: 237). For example, they leave intact the assumption that capitalism is a gender-neutral system, and that the ability to 'freely' exchange labour for a wage is universal.

This suggestion – that capitalism is patriarchal – opens up all sorts of possibilities regarding the gendered operations of the labour market. We might ask, for instance, whether the construction of men and women as different sorts of 'workers' has any other consequences for the gendered operations of the labour market beyond already established and well-documented patterns of gender differentiation (such as various forms of gender segregation and the wages gap). This is important, for if capitalism *is* patriarchal, then we might expect, as Acker (1990) suggests, that the labour market is far more fundamentally gendered than previous analyses have suggested. 'Patriarchal capitalism' suggests a gendering of the labour market which is far more embedded in labour market practices than the dual systems approaches imply, and such gendering may involve a great deal more than the control of women's access to wages. For instance, patriarchal relations in the labour market may not simply operate to determine who fills the places in a hierarchy of workers created by a (gender-neutral) capitalism (cf. Hartmann and Walby), but the hierarchy itself (in the first instance) may be patriarchal. We thus need to ask whether capitalism may be constructed as patriarchal in even more ways than those suggested by Pateman *et al.* Do other factors, as well as the gendered structuring of the family, contribute to the sex-specific construction of women's labour and locate women differently from men in relation to the labour market? From the point of view of the concerns of this book, may sexuality itself contribute to such a structuring? We must also ask if there are processes or sets of social relations *internal* to the labour market which contribute to the specific construction of women's labour. In what other ways does the patriarchal structuring of capitalism express itself in the labour market? The notion of a free proletarian worker may have been exposed as a gendered category, but what of other labour market categories, such as 'production'? Might this practice not also be gendered?

The new developments in feminist thinking about the labour market by Mies and Cockburn, taken together with the broader developments in feminist theorizing outlined here (by Delphy and Leonard, Pateman and Acker), clearly raise some fairly fundamental issues. But despite the significance of these developments on the gendering of work, sexuality *still* continues to be treated in a problematic fashion in many feminist analyses of the labour market, including those studies which have made an explicit attempt to consider the relationship between sexuality and employment.

Sexuality and employment: some recent studies

Since the late 1980s, a number of studies have been completely or partially dedicated to exploring the relationship between sexuality and employment. These form part of a developing body of literature concerned with the significance of sexuality for employment relations and/or the structuring of organizations. This literature quite rightly points out how sexuality has previously been ignored and/or marginalized in both labour market theory and organization theory, but despite this recognition, and a stated desire to expose sexuality as significant in the shaping of the labour market and organizations, these analyses nevertheless operate with either a taken-for-granted and/or a limited view of the construction of sexuality.

The most straightforward example of a recent study which does not problematize sexuality but rather treats it in a taken-for-granted manner, is Hearn and Parkin's (1987) study of sexuality in organizations, in which they suggest that 'organizational sexuality' can be understood as a by-product of what they define as (ungendered) capitalist labour market processes. In their argument, they simply take male-dominated heterosexual relations for granted saying, for instance, that the sexual harassment of women by men in employment can be understood as a product of alienating work conditions. Such conditions incite men to harass. They base this claim on an assertion that sexual harassment is particularly endemic in industries characterized by alienating work conditions, where men lack control over what they produce and the act of production.

But this argument is highly dubious. It assumes either that it is only men who experience alienation from their work, or that it is only men who react to these conditions. However, ethnographic studies of women's experiences of the labour market (see, e.g. Pollert 1981; Westwood 1984), which have revealed that women develop different strategies in alienating work conditions, clearly problematize both these assumptions. Women both experience and 'react' to alienation. This clearly undermines the argument that the sexual harassment of women by men within the workplace can be understood in terms of alienation, because it does not explain the gender specificity of harassment (that it is men who do it to women). If both men and women experience alienation, why should this lead men, and only men, to harass? In any case, this whole argument is constructed upon an empirical claim that sexual harassment is particularly evident in industries characterized by alienating work conditions, and that there is a simple relationship between the degree of harassment women are subjected to and the degree of alienation men experience in the labour process. This simply ignores empirical findings on sexual harassment (see below).

As well as explaining sexual harassment by alienation, Hearn and Parkin also attempt to reduce other 'instances' of sexuality in organizations to what they see as capitalist labour market processes. For instance, they see displays of pornography in the workplace by men as also deriving from men's boredom with their work: pornography is a way to escape boredom (Hearn and Parkin 1987: 89). Alternatively, they suggest that the labour process can alienate men from their sexuality – men who work night shifts may have a 'disrupted' sexual life outside of the workplace – and this constitutes an alienation which may lead men to refuse to work such shifts. Or again, the gender division of labour (which itself is posited to be an outcome of capitalist processes, since Hearn and Parkin believe women form a reserve army of labour for capital) is also seen to produce 'organization sexuality'. They argue that gender divisions of labour are reinforced by gender divisions of authority and power, both of which are expressed through organizational hierarchies, and hierarchical organizational structures in turn construct hierarchical interpersonal relations between people, including sexual relations. Hearn and Parkin (1987: 92) thus suggest, for example, that the higher valuation of men than women in organizations parallels the tendency to value men's sexuality more highly than that of women. In this rather tortuous argument, men's sexuality is associated with the properties of more highly valued labour and higher positions in the hierarchy, with, for example, control, activity, physical power and emotional distance.

What is particularly problematic about Hearn and Parkin's argument is that in reducing sexuality to a by-product of capitalist processes, they simultaneously naturalize and essentialize hetero-sexual relations. For instance, when they assume that the sexual harassment of women by men is produced by alienation, or that men's sexuality is valued more highly than women's in organiz-ations because women constitute a reserve army of labour for capital, they assume male-dominated sexuality. This applies to all their other instances of 'organization sexuality' as well. Reducing sexual harassment to alienation completely obscures the ways in which, through sexual harassment, men control women (see MacKinnon 1979; Stanko 1985, 1988) and, moreover, they take men's ability and power and desire to sexually harass women to be simply a characteristic of men's sexuality. Similarly, their argu-ment that male-dominated sexuality is an outcome of, or can be 'read off' from, gender divisions created by capital, makes the same naturalistic assumptions. Why should capitalist hierarchies call into being a sexuality in which women are sexually exploited by men? They simply assume that sexuality will be male-dominated. They thus not only ignore the ways in which patriarchal agents actively produce and maintain gendered divisions of labour within organizations (Hartmann 1979; Cockburn 1983, 1985, 1991; Summerfield 1984; Walby 1986), but also the way this occurs within sexuality (see Tabet 1987, 1989; Holland et al. 1990).

While Hearn and Parkin's analysis of sexuality and employment is clearly problematic, some of the other more recent studies which have attempted to unravel and understand the operation of sexuality in the labour market raise a different set of problems. Pringle (1989a, 1989b), for example, has attempted to avoid the difficulties associated with the exclusion of sexuality from feminist analyses of the labour market through an analysis of the ways in which sexuality (and indeed the whole of gender) is discursively and symbolically produced in the workplace. This analysis takes place primarily through an exploration of the cultural meanings embodied in occupations and the formation of gendered workplace subjectivities. However, she too, like other feminist labour market theorists, does not escape the separation of the sexual from processes of the gendering of the labour market.

Thus, in her study of the boss–secretary relationship, through a series of interviews with 'pairs' of bosses and secretaries and a historical study of the cultural construction of the category 'secretary', Pringle shows how the power relations between bosses and secretaries relate to the operation of a number of (often overlapping) discourses based on sexual and family imagery which locate bosses and secretaries in a number of different subject positions. For example, the operation of a master–slave discourse is identified by Pringle, where the boss is located as the subject (as the dominator and controller) and the secretary as the object (as, for example, a subordinate wife or attractive mistress who must carry out personal services such as shopping, washing, acting as a hostess for clients and be available for the boss and submit to his wishes whenever it is required). A mother/nanny–son discourse is also identified as structuring the boss–secretary relationship. Here the secretary is positioned as the subject (as mother, dominating wife or paid servant who must protect, provide emotional support and anticipate the needs of the boss) and the boss as the object (as the helpless/naughty child). More 'modern' boss–secretary relations are located as structured by a discourse of reciprocity, where equality and 'teamwork' are emphasized. Despite the supposed gender-neutrality of this discourse (where subject and object positions are open), Pringle shows how in this relationship bosses may use the language of reciprocity but still require 'their' secretaries to meet their personal needs. Indeed, Pringle shows how both elements of the master–slave and mother/nanny–son discourses may operate between bosses and secretaries where there is surface commitment to teamwork, reciprocity and equality. Pringle also provides some evidence to suggest that boss–secretary relationships may be organized in terms of a father–daughter discourse where, for instance, bosses not only control secretaries at work, but also gain a detailed knowledge of, and seek control of, their private lives.

Pringle argues that the operation of these discourses is central to the formation of workplace power relations between men and women. In particular, she argues that these discourses construct secretaries exclusively in familial and sexual terms – as office wives/mistresses, mothers/nannies or daughters. As a consequence, the variety of gendered subject and object positions produced through these discourses allows bosses to establish a variety of forms of sexual and familial control over secretaries (including control of the use of their labour, their appearance, and the organization of their private lives). In addition, Pringle suggests that because secretaries are exclusively symbolically constructed in familial and sexual terms, the only forms of workplace authority secretaries may claim are those which operate in relation to their subject positions as office wives/mistresses, mothers/nannies or daughters. In contrast, while bosses may be located as masters, fathers or helpless/naughty children, their workplace authority is not dependent on their subject or object positions in relation to their secretaries:

> While men may be perceived as husbands or fathers, their authority at work rarely depends on this. Though they are necessarily engaged in power relations with their secretaries, the outcome will only marginally affect their power within the organisation.
>
> (Pringle 1989a: 51)

In stressing the cultural and symbolic construction of occupations and identifying the formation of workplace identities as key for the construction of power relations between men and women in the sphere of employment, Pringle's analysis certainly breaks away from many of the traditional concerns of feminist thinking about the labour market. But despite this, her account shares some of the same characteristics found in the traditional accounts. Specifically, she reproduces many of the same old ambiguities regarding the relationship of sexuality to the 'economic', and especially to men's economic advantage in the labour market.

For instance, while Pringle shows that women's cultural identities may be exclusively structured in sexual terms (the 'attractive mistress' or 'sexy secretary'), the issue of the relationship between these sexualized workplace identities and the processes of formation of men's economic and other advantages in the labour market remains unclear. This is the case despite the fact that throughout her analysis she argues for the centrality of discursive and symbolic power relations for the gendered organization of work. But it is not clear from her account how the symbolic and the discursive processes she identifies relate to such organization. Thus, although Pringle certainly provides lots of evidence of men's (bosses') appropriation of women's (secretaries') labour (including demands for huge amounts of unpaid overtime, the entertainment of guests/clients and other forms of personal servicing such as shopping and washing), it is not clear from her analysis how the symbolic positioning of bosses (for example, as master, father or naughty child) provide the conditions through which these various forms of work can be extorted from secretaries. That is, Pringle does not show how men's cultural and symbolic power over women produces power to control and appropriate women's labour (Adkins and Lury 1994).

In her recent study of men's resistance to women's equality in organizations, Cockburn (1991) has also turned her attention to sexuality. At first sight, as in the case of Pringle, Cockburn's research appears to open up feminist thinking on the labour market, especially since she does discuss the pervasive operation of sexuality, emotions and bodies in the labour market. Indeed, she claims that 'sexuality, emotions, and the representation and use of bodies enters into [organizational] ... life and labour processes' (Cockburn 1991: 150). But, as with Pringle, in Cockburn's account the relationship between sexuality (and bodies and emotions) and processes of the gendering of the labour market is rather hazy.

For example, Cockburn suggests sexuality may enter into the labour process via employers' exploitation of sexuality for profit: 'the "sexy" uniform of a club waitress exploits for profit both her female sexuality and the male sexuality of the client' (Cockburn 1991: 149). She says that using sexuality in this way means it may constitute a force of production. But while this certainly implies that sexuality may indeed enter into the labour process, the full implications of the sexual constituting a force of production are nevertheless not addressed in terms of gender (Adkins and Lury

1994). That is to say, Cockburn only discusses the significance of sexuality constituting a force of production in terms of capitalist production. She sees such work as being exploited only for profit. She does not consider the possibility that the appropriation of sexuality in the labour market may be a gendered phenomenon, nor does she consider how the exploitation of women's sexuality may relate to the gendering of the labour market itself – how the exploitation of women's sexuality may relate to, for example, the construction of economic power relations between men and women workers, to men's control of women's labour in co-worker relations.

Cockburn also records a number of other ways in which emotions, sexuality and bodies permeate the workplace. For example, she discusses how a retail company's advertising and shop windows are full of 'idealised, "attractive" women, men and children wearing the company's clothes, using the company's consumer durables' (Cockburn 1991: 150), and how the same company runs an annual beauty contest for employees. She also discusses the ways in which employees may be required to wear uniforms which involve a deliberate sexualizing or desexualizing of the body; how heterosexual culture is actively produced in the labour market and how lesbian desire is censored out of workplaces; how offices may be deliberately open-plan to avoid 'hanky-panky'; and the pervasive operation of sexualized discourses throughout organizations. She thus notes a whole host of ways in which workplace life is sexualized. But, as with Pringle, what stands out from her account is a lack of attention to the relationship between these instances of sexuality operating in the workplace and the gendered structuring of the labour market itself. While idealized images of attractive women may be in circulation, and lesbian desire may be censored out of the workplace via the active production of a heterosexual culture, Cockburn does not address the issue of how such images or culture may be of significance in terms of, for instance, men's power over women to claim greater access to occupational resources and skills (Adkins and Lury 1994).

Pringle's and Cockburn's analyses certainly stand out from early feminist accounts of the labour market in their recognition that 'sexuality is everywhere' in the workplace (Pringle 1989b). But although they recognize sexuality to be ubiquitous, their lack of attention to its relationship with the labour market, means it remains as distinct from the labour market as in the 'old' accounts. Ironically, although early feminist analyses are critiqued for peripheralizing the significance of (what were defined as) non-economic or non-material processes (such as sexuality and culture), more recent analyses which have attempted to 'pull in' previously marginalized processes have in fact upheld the differentiation of sexuality from the processes of the gendering of the labour market. However, as will be made clear in later chapters, this continued differentiation is problematic in that it precludes the possibility of the development of a full understanding of the processes of gendering of the labour market. In particular, it precludes a consideration of the gendered organization of the 'economic': of the ways in which sexual identities available to men and women in the workplace, for instance, relate to the gendered nature of the very fabric of the labour market – to (gendered) economic relations.

What also stands out from Cockburn's and Pringle's analyses is their treatment of sexuality itself, and in particular their separation of 'coercive' and 'non-coercive' heterosexuality (Adkins 1992b). Both agree that 'men control women not only through rape or through forcing them to do what they want [them] to do but through definitions of pleasure and selfhood' (Pringle 1989b: 165, cited in Cockburn 1991: 158). But in her analysis of her material on secretaries, Pringle still assumes that heterosexuality is only male-dominated and unequal whan men impose sexual attention on women by force. This is evident in her thesis that feminists' focus on the coercive elements of sexuality in relation to the workplace (notably through their focus on sexual harassment) has been detrimental to a consideration of the positive elements of sexuality for women. She argues:

> Rather than assuming ... that secretaries are always the pathetic victims of sexual harassment, it might be possible to consider the power and pleasure they currently get out of their interactions with people and how they get what they want on their own terms.
>
> (Pringle 1989a: 101-102)

What is important here is that Pringle is not simply making a distinction between different kinds of heterosexual interactions (i.e. coercive and non-coercive). Rather, she is assuming that these are constituted differently; that they are different sorts of heterosexuality. Coercive interactions make women powerless victims, while non-coercive heterosexuality may afford women power, pleasure and excitement. Coercive and non-coercive heterosexual practices are, in other words, presented as if they are unconnected with each other.

Cockburn also makes the same distinction between different sorts of heterosexual practice. She sees the sexual harassment of women by men in employment as a 'male intervention for the assertion of power' (Cockburn 1991: 142), and she shows how men's sexual banter and sexual innuendo act as a means of control of women. But she then goes on to say that 'sexual harassment shows only the negative side of organization sexuality' (p. 152). On the 'positive' side, she points to the opportunities that employment affords both men and women for sociability, since 'work can be a path to pleasure too' (p. 151). Hence, she says, 'women as well as men have a stake in the degree of openness and sociability in the organization' (p. 152). Although Cockburn is at pains to point out that sexual pleasure, sociability and openness are all risky for women compared with men because of the power relations of heterosexuality, she none the less still sees these power relations as being substantially negotiable and flexible for women – and certainly so compared with directly coercive sexual relations with men. This is evident in her concluding comments on sexuality and employment, where she agrees with Pringle that strategies for change involve:

> ... being bold in knowing and asserting our likes as well as our dislikes. Opposition to sexual harassment is only one component of a sexual politics of the workplace. It needs to be supplemented with analyses of the ways in which sexual pleasure might be used to disrupt male rationality and to empower women.
>
> (Cockburn 1991: 159)

Here, like Pringle, Cockburn clearly sees heterosexual relations that are not 'harassment' as voluntary, and even as a potential threat to men's power. Sexual harassment requires direct opposition, but definitions of sexual pleasure are so fluid that their meaning can be subverted by women to such an extent that they can empower them in the workplace. For both Cockburn and Pringle, then, coercive sexuality is male-dominated; but non-coercive heterosexuality, while it may be subject to the power relations of gender, is not necessarily constituted by or through gendered power relations.

This argument is clearly very different from the radical feminist analyses of sexuality discussed earlier in this chapter, which stress the continuum between 'coercive' and 'non-coercive' heterosexuality and the ways in which male dominance structures both 'sorts'. Indeed, this literature stresses the difficulties with making such a distinction (see in particular Kelly 1988). We shall see in later chapters, however, that Cockburn and Pringle have a rather limited view of the social structuring of heterosexuality in the workplace and, moreover, that this limited understanding is a direct outcome of their continued differentiation of the 'sexual' from the 'economic'.

The sex industry and sexual harassment at work

While sexual and economic relations have continued to be separated out in feminist analyses of the labour market, two areas of feminist concern have seen rather more engagement, namely accounts of women and children in the 'sex industry' (i.e. in prostitution and the production of pornography) and the sexual harassment of women at work.

Some feminist accounts of prostitution stress a woman's right to choose to be a prostitute, arguing it is simply a stigmatized job, a rational choice by women to exchange sexual services for money, and the best-paying job choice available for those who could otherwise earn only very poor wages.[12] Others stress the exploitation and abuse of women associated with prostitution and the production of pornography: the enormous sums of money made by sex-industry entrepreneurs and the coercive role and practices of men as pimps and procurers. They foreground the power relations of heterosexuality as key to an understanding of the situation of women who work in the sex industry. Kelly (1990: 34), for example, argues that '[pornography] objectifies women and celebrates coercive heterosexuality. It is women and children who have the least choices, who are exploited by, and in, the sex industry internationally'.

The latter group maintain a critical distance from the notion of 'sex-work', which is much used by the former. They believe it downplays the prevalence of coercive exploitation of women's sexuality by over-emphasizing a 'free' exchange of sexual services for money. They argue this obscures the ways in which many women are physically coerced into working in the sex industry (Kelly 1985, 1990). Indeed, one US-based campaign group, WHISPER (Women Hurt In Systems of Prostitution Engaged in Revolt), argues that the concept 'sex-work' should be abandoned because rather than being a form of work, 'sex-work' should be understood as a form of violence against women (Giobbe 1990).

Both sides agree that many of the problems of prostitution derive from its illegality, which exposes women to police intervention, opens the doors to exploitation by profiteers, and increases the risks of violence from clients and pimps. All stress the connections between the situation of women 'sex-workers' and the situation of women who are not involved in the sex industry, often arguing that prostitution and marriage are connected, even though they are presented as opposed to each other (see, e.g. Hamilton 1912; Guillaumin 1981; Tabet 1987; Alexander 1988). Far from being opposites, or discrete phenomena, marital relations and sex-industry relations are both instances of the physical use of women by men, involving women exchanging sex for money, gifts or maintenance.

Colette Guillaumin (1981: 10), for example, has said how marriage and prostitution 'confirm each other in their expression of the appropriation of women as a class'. Prostitution involves a physical usage of women by men which is limited to sexual usage by sale, whereas marriage involves a much broader physical usage of women (including sexual usage), to the extent that wives do not own their own bodies.

Guillaumin suggests the physical appropriation of wives is evident in the way that husbands are free to use their own bodies as they please. Men may, for example, use prostitutes, but such a usage has not constituted grounds for adultery or divorce in France. For wives, on the other hand, any sexual relations with someone who is not her husband *always* constitutes grounds for divorce. Guillaumin (1981: 10) argues this is a clear demonstration of the physical appropriation of wives: 'One can say, a woman must not forget that she is appropriated, and that, as her husband's property, she obviously cannot do what she wants with her own body'. She points out that this not only demonstrates how wives' bodies do not belong to them personally, but rather belong to their husbands, but also that this is the reason why there is no prostitution for women: 'There can be no prostitution for those who do not own their own bodies' (Guillaumin 1981: 11). Prostitution and marriage both exist, in Guillaumin's view, because of the physical appropriation of women. They are the flip sides of the same coin: wives and prostitutes are both subject to physical sexual appropriation, an appropriation which is possible because women do not own their bodies in the same way as men.

WHISPER, too, suggests that the situation of the sex-worker reveals the situation of all women:

> Prostitution isn't like anything else. Rather, everything else is like prostitution because it is the model for women's condition . . . the prostitute symbolizes the value of women in society. She is paradigmatic of women's social, sexual and economic subordination in that her status is the basic unit by which all women's value is measured and to which all women can be reduced. The treatment that a man pays to inflict on the most despised women – prostitutes – sets the standard by which he may treat the women under his control – his wife and his daughters.
>
> (Giobbe 1990: 76–7)

Such analyses of the connections between wives and prostitutes and of the connections between the situation of women 'sex-workers' and women more generally, raise important issues for any consideration of sexuality and the labour market. In particular, the connections that Guillaumin spells out suggest that one reason why women may not be 'workers' in the same way as men is because of a physical sexual appropriation of women (see also Pateman 1988). Or, to put it another way, the structuring of heterosexuality and 'male sex right' may constitute a particular form of the sex-specific exploitation of women's labour. Thus, such an appropriation may form a way in which (as Rich and Raymond suggest) heterosexuality contributes to the control of women's labour.

Clearly, however, for such a sequence to be spelt out, connections must be drawn and explicated between women 'sex-workers' and women who are wage-workers but who do not work in the sex industry. Moreover, it would require asking such questions as: How is such a physical sexual appropriation of women effected in the labour market? What are the conditions through which such an appropriation is produced? How does it relate to other forms of inequalities between men and women in the labour market, such as men's economic advantage over women?

The other strand of feminist work which attempts to address some of the connections between sexual and economic relations is that concerned with the sexual harassment of women in employment. A number of studies and analyses of the sexual harassment of women have been carried out (e.g. Farley 1978, Hadjifotiou 1983; Leeds TUCRIC 1983), but here I shall focus on just two, those by Stanko (1988) and MacKinnon (1979). Both explicitly attempt to unravel the nature, form(s) and importance of the relationship between sexuality and labour market processes for an understanding of the construction of women's position within the workplace, through a specific focus on sexual harassment.

Stanko has not only documented the pervasiveness of sexual harassment in the labour market (see in particular Stanko 1985), but has also explored the significance of harassment for one distinctive feature of the labour market, gendered occupational segregation (Stanko 1988). The latter analysis places sexual harassment in the context of men's dominance over women, where sexual objectification – 'a process over which women have had little, if any control' (Stanko 1988: 91) – permeates the workplace, as all other social locations. She defines sexual harassment broadly as 'unwanted sexual attention', including behaviour ranging from visual leering to rape. But while the forms of harassing bahaviour may vary, they have a unified effect: they all serve to transform women into sexual objects.

With harassment defined and placed within the context of gendered power relations, Stanko then goes on to explore its significance within the labour market. She shows how women experience humiliation, self-blame, anger, loss of self-confidence, and a drop in job performance levels as a result of unwanted/imposed sexual attention. She suggests sexual harassment has a complex twist as regards the labour market. There are very concrete effects and economic consequences: some women resign, others are transferred or demoted, and some lose their jobs if they do not cooperate with sexual advances. More-over, few women win cases of unfair dismissal resulting from sexual harassment (for documentation of sexual harassment cases, see MacKinnon 1979).

Both women's experiences and the economic consequences of sexual harassment at the workplace suggest that sexual processes are a powerful force in the construction of women's position in the labour market. As Stanko (1988: 93) suggests: 'While complex and complicated in our everyday lives, the configuration of gender, power and sexuality poses particular problems when they locate themselves at work'. She attempts to address this issue of the relationship between sexual harassment and the labour market through a focus on occupational segregation by gender. She suggests, for example, that sexuality may be produced and reproduced via occupational segregation. In particular, solidarity between men within segregated occupations may be built 'by drawing upon what is assumed to be a mutual heterosexual interest in sexuality' (Stanko 1988: 94), such solidarity being fostered through the sexual objectification of women workers. Thus, men's economic advantage in the labour market may be enhanced through the sexual objectification of women.

But what are the processes which lead to this outcome? Stanko seeks to understand the interrelationship of sexual harassment and occupational segregation (that is, the extent to which sexual harassment produces or reproduces segregation at the workplace) and explores this via the 'levels' of harassment in different occupations. Arguing against the notion that the rates of reported harassment equal the extent of such behaviour (cf. Hearn and Parkin), Stanko shows how and why reportage is an inadequate indicator of behaviour. Her own evidence suggests that women entering 'non-traditional' areas of employment, especially previously all-male occupations, are more likely to report sexual harassment than women in 'traditional' areas of employment, because the former may assume that they are employed 'on a par' with men and that harassment will not be part of their experience.[13] In contrast, women in 'traditional' areas of employment, such as those in service and care-giving jobs, have less 'right' to complain about sexual harassment and, as a consequence, are less likely to report harassing behaviour:

Women in traditional employment may have already found
a number of strategies to negotiate men's behaviour. They
may also assume that being annoyed or bothered by men in
these jobs is part of the job.

(Stanko 1988: 96)

Stanko goes on to suggest that women who work in traditional
women's occupations are routinely sexualized as 'part of the job'.
This sexualization, she argues, serves to eroticize women's subordination in the labour market, which may account for the ways in
which secretaries are turned into 'office wives' (see Benet 1972;
Pringle 1989a, 1989b) and waitresses into sexual servicers (see
Spradley and Mann 1975).

Stanko suggests that the endemic nature of harassment, and in
particular the experiences of women who enter 'non-traditional'
areas of employment where the majority of the occupational
places are filled by men, supports her earlier claims that such
relations serve to bond men. Displays of heterosexual interest are
central to such bonding, and making men's working environments
the site of such bonding makes them still more firmly part of their
territory. Such solidarity between men supports and promotes the
sexualization of women. Sexual harassment is thus a strategy used
by men to protect their territories (occupations) and hence to defend
their material benefits over women: 'We know women quit jobs
because they are leaving harassing situations; do they choose jobs to
minimise their confrontations with harassers?' (Stanko 1988: 98).

While Stanko argues for a recognition of the importance of
sexual harassment in constructing men's advantage over women in
the labour market, what stands out from her account is an
ambiguity with regard to the degree of importance of sexual
harassment in organizing segregation. At times she seems almost to
be suggesting that sexual harassment explains occupational segregation, for example in her discussion of the 'territoriality' of
occupations (that is, the use of occupational space for men's
organization and closure, through the sexual objectification of
women, to the extent that women 'choose' occupations to
minimize confrontations with harassers). Here there seems to be an
implicit suggestion that occupational 'spaces' become closed to
women as a direct outcome of sexuality, in which case gender

segregation itself is seen as to some extent to be produced by sexuality.

At other points in her analysis, however, Stanko implies that sexual harassment is somehow imposed on top of already constituted gendered labour market divisions: that it serves simply to reinforce or maintain these divisions. Such an argument is to be found, for instance, in her discussion of women employed in traditional occupations, where she implies that the sexualization of women within these occupations, while acting to reinforce women's subordinate position, is none the less independent of the production of gender segregation (or the production of women's location in 'traditional women's jobs'). Women's position within such occupations is, she says, formed prior to processes of sexualization. Thus secretaries *become* office wives, and waitresses are *turned into* sexual servicers. In other words, women in these occupations are sexualized by men *after* the formation of gender segregation. In such cases, the production of segregation and sexuality are held to be separate. Indeed, the sexualization of women in these jobs is almost presented as an outcome of women occupying 'women's jobs'; and men's ability to sexualize and harass women in the labour market is thus produced through segregation.

Such a separation of occupational segregation and sexuality is also found in Stanko's (1988: 99) suggestion that 'women need to keep in mind how to combat sexual harassment along with economic segregation'. Once again sexuality is held to be outside of the processes involved in the production of gender segregation (which Stanko here suggests are economic relations). In this part of her analysis, sexual relations are seen to be far more peripheral to the production of gender divisions in the labour market than they are in her discussion of 'territoriality'. Instead of producing economic divisions, sexuality here only serves to reproduce them. Thus economic relations are given priority over those of sexuality in the formation of occupational segregation.

In the light of the varying degrees of significance which Stanko attributes to sexuality for the production of gender segregation in the labour market and men's economic advantage over women, it is interesting that MacKinnon (1979) argues that the sexual harassment of women is both productive and reproductive of gendered labour market divisions. Within the latter's analysis (in which her position is quite different from that found in her more recent work), she describes the major dynamic of sexual harassment within the labour market as one where there is a reciprocal enforcement of two inequalities, one sexual and the other material (MacKinnon 1979: 1). When these operate together, the cumulative sanction is 'particularly potent ... society legitimizes male sexual dominance of women and employer's control of workers' (ibid.). She suggests the defining context for understanding the significance of the sexual harassment of women workers is thus one of 'employer–employee relations (given women's position in the labour force) and the relationship between the sexes in . . . society as a whole' (MacKinnon 1979: 2).

Within the labour market, where these two systems of domination interlock, MacKinnon suggests their meaning takes on particular potency and significance. It means, for instance, that if women do not respond to sexual advances from men superiors (and the vertical segregation of women in the labour market means that in by far the majority of cases women's superiors will be men), or if they do not comply with advances from men co-workers or men customers, employment retaliation may follow. She points out that acts of harassment always have material coercion behind them. These may remain 'implicit in the employer's position to apply it. Or it may be explicitly communicated through, for example, firing for non-compliance or retention conditioned upon continued sexual compliance' (MacKinnon 1979: 2). In the context of the labour market, MacKinnon suggests that the most straightforward example of the way in which sexual and economic domination interlock is 'put out or get out' (ibid.).

But how exactly do these power structures interact, and how can we explain women's position in the labour market through this relationship? In attempting to answer these questions, MacKinnon initially concentrates on sexuality, recognizing the sexual harassment of women as a key mechanism through which women's structurally inferior position relative to men is maintained in the labour market:

Sexual harassment exemplifies and promotes employment practices which disadvantage women in work (especially occupational segregation), and sexual practices which intimately degrade and objectify women.

(MacKinnon 1979: 7)

She suggests that sexual harassment 'promotes' the disadvantage of women workers in this way, in that it occurs not only because women occupy inferior job positions and job roles, but also because harassment works to keep women in such positions: 'Sexual harassment . . . uses and helps create women's structurally inferior status' (MacKinnon 1979: 9). Rigid gender divisions in the labour market should therefore be understood as both created and reinforced by sexual harassment. Acting as a closed system of 'social predation', sexual harassment builds powerlessness from powerlessness:

> Working women are defined and survive by defining themselves as sexually accessible and economically exploitable. Because they are economically vulnerable, they are sexually exposed, because they must be sexually accessible, they are always at risk. In this perspective sexual harassment is less 'epidemic' than endemic.
>
> (MacKinnon 1979: 55)

The power relations of sexuality and capitalism interlock in the context of the labour market to specify women's position, keeping women sexually in thrall to men, at the bottom of the labour market. Women become jointly exploited in the workplace through both their sexuality and their work, when the work demands placed on women become sexual requirements of work. Women's sexuality becomes 'a condition of her subsistence, its delivery part of the definition of her productive activity' (MacKinnon 1979: 216). Sexual harassment acts as a key mechanism in this more general process, sedimenting women's second-class status both sexually and economically:

> . . . sexual harassment expresses and reinforces a sex-stereotyped perspective that women hired for 'women's jobs' are to be at the service of men in every way, are fair game for male sexual advances, and owe men sexual liberties – all of which works to their disadvantage as women workers.
>
> (MacKinnon 1979: 209)

The sexual harassment of women within the labour market thus works to systematically disadvantage women in employment, for it is an abuse of economic power by men, but it operates in a structural situation in which women can be (and are) systematically subordinated to men sexually and in other ways. MacKinnon (1979: 220) concludes that:

> Sexual harassment at work connects the jobs most women do (in which a major part of their work is to be there for men) with the structure of sexual relations (in which their role is also to be there for men) with the denigrated economic status women as a gender occupy throughout society.

What is perhaps most striking about MacKinnon's analysis is that while she does argue to some extent that sexual harassment produces gender divisions within the labour market, she does not demonstrate or explicate this. She sees women's position in the labour market as providing men with structural economic power in relation to women, and it is this power which men abuse when they sexually harass women (which is why sexual harassment is endemic, since men as a group hold more powerful positions within the hierarchy of jobs than women). But throughout her analysis, MacKinnon assumes women's position within the labour market is formed through these economic relations, and not through sexual harassment.

This assumption can be found, for instance, in the way in which women's denigrated economic status, although it is said to be formed through the structure of general relations between men and women, nevertheless is held to be a separate structure from sexual harassment. Sexual harassment is an outcome of one particular form of these general relations: men's economic power in relation to women. Sexual harassment is 'possible' to the extent that the 'work demands placed on women become the sexual requirements of work', only because of these more general relations between men and women. In particular, acts of sexual harassment in the labour market always have behind them economic coercion. Sexual harassment therefore does not produce these relations, but rather (according to MacKinnon) it is an outcome of them. This can be seen for example in her claim that when women are hired for 'women's jobs', sexual harassment enforces and reinforces the perspective that these women are to be at the service of men in every way. Here sexual harassment is seen to maintain the general relation in which women exist in relation to men, while these relations themselves mean that women are hired for 'women's jobs'. In this way, sexual harassment is held to be separate from, and peripheral to, the formation of women's position in the labour market: it is imposed on top an already structured labour market.

However, what is interesting about MacKinnon's analysis is not so much that she fails to demonstrate that sexual harassment produces gender divisions within the labour market, but rather the manner in which she incurs this failure. For her failure is tied to the use of the concept of sexual harassment itself. In her analysis, MacKinnon defines harassment (as indeed does Stanko) as separate from economic relations – as non-economic. The labour market, on the other hand, is defined as an economic entity. Within the labour market, gender divisions – and in particular gender segregation – are seen as a product of economic relations. Clearly, when MacKinnon tries to use these definitions to attempt to argue that sexual harassment can produce economic divisions, it is a fruitless task. How can what are defined as non-economic relations (sexual harassment) be constitutive of an entity (the labour market) which is defined as purely economic? By locating harassment as non-economic, and the production of gender divisions within the labour market as economic, the significance of sexual harassment for the production of such divisions will always be assessed as secondary to economic relations. It may 'reinforce' or 'express' such relations, but it cannot produce them.

This separation of sexuality from the labour market – by defining the labour market as economic and sexuality as non-economic – is, as we have seen, one of the characteristics of feminist labour market theory, both past and present. In Stanko's analysis, however, the significance of sexuality for gendered labour market divisions is more ambiguous: sexuality is seen both to maintain and to produce gendered work relations. Moreover, unlike MacKinnon, Stanko goes some way towards actually demonstrating the manner in which sexuality may produce such divisions. What is particularly significant here (in the light of the problems that MacKinnon experiences when attempting to argue that sexual harassment produces labour market divisions) is that the moment when Stanko's analysis begins to suggest that sexuality may produce gendered labour market divisions, is precisely the moment at which she moves away from a dominant assumption (in both her own and MacKinnon's analysis) that 'sexuality' in the labour market equals, or is synonymous with, sexual harassment.

As has been seen, the point at which Stanko's analysis implies that 'sexuality' does more than maintain gendered divisions occurs during her discussion of territoriality. Here she suggests that sexuality may serve as an organizing principle in the labour market, that it may promote solidarity between men through which men may organize to exclude and segregate women workers from and within the labour market. What this part of her analysis implies is that sexuality may play a significant part in the production of gendered 'economic' divisions. With this suggestion, she moves away from assuming that sexuality only operates within the labour market in relation to the sexual harassment of women workers. Instead, she opens up the possibility of sexuality operating in a far broader sense – as a principle of organization. As an outcome of this break, the significance to be attached to sexuality in the production of gender divisions changes dramatically. Instead of merely maintaining these divisions, it becomes – to some extent at least – productive of them. This calls all manner of aspects of the relationship of sexuality and the labour market into question. Most significantly, it suggests that forms of control of women's labour within the labour market may be produced through aspects of sexuality (Rich 1983; Raymond 1986). However, within Stanko's own analysis there are insufficient grounds for making such a claim; the connection is implied rather than being fully explicated or explored.

Taken together, however, MacKinnon's and Stanko's analyses open up all sorts of issues which require exploration with regard to the interplay between sexuality and the labour market. Their analyses raise questions concerning the exact significance of sexuality in the dynamics of the labour market. Does sexuality maintain gendered structural divisions (most particularly occupational segregation)? Or, does it actually produce these divisions? In addition, the reason why MacKinnon fails to demonstrate that sexuality (or more precisely sexual harassment) produces such divisions, and the way in which Stanko's analysis hesitates on the verge of suggesting that sexuality may be productive of them, raises questions about the exact nature of 'sexuality' in the labour market. Does sexuality operate as non-economic or economic? Is it

'confined' to practices of harassment? Or, is sexuality an organizing principle of the whole labour market? Moreover, if the latter is
the case, does this imply that men and women are not the same
kinds of 'workers' in the labour market because of heterosexuality
(Pateman 1988)?

In many respects, Stanko's and MacKinnon's accounts both
provide more questions than answers. But nevertheless, their
evidence regarding sexual harassment, especially their work on the
economic consequences of harassment for women workers, does
establish that 'sexuality', whether producing or 'merely' reproduc-
ing gender divisions, plays a significant role in the gendered
dynamics of the labour market. They therefore break with many
of the analyses considered earlier, which accord sexuality little
significance in the operations of the labour market, or which avoid
the issue of the interaction or the overlap between the 'sexual' and
the 'economic'.

In reviewing the current state of feminist thinking about the
labour market, and in particular by interrogating the place and
status accorded to sexuality within this thinking, this chapter has
raised a whole series of issues which are significant for any consideration of the relationship between sexuality and the gendered
operations of the labour market. These have included issues
regarding the form sexual relations may take in the labour market.
Are they expressed in economic or non-economic forms? Is sexual
harassment the primary expression of sexuality in the labour
market? Or, is it possible that heterosexual social relations may
somehow be implicated in the very organization of the labour
market, and therefore that heterosexuality may be involved in the
patriarchal construction of capitalism? All these issues will be
returned to in Chapters 4 and 5. Chapter 3 considers the issue of the
relationship between family work and labour market work.

Notes

1 See also Gordon 1972; Edwards *et al.* 1975; Rubery 1978; Edwards
   1979 and Craig *et al.* 1982, 1985.
2 Beechey (1987), Pringle (1989a) and Glucksman (1990) provide
   discussions of the problems associated with this model of employment.

3 See, for example, McNally (1979) on secretaries, Crompton and Jones (1984) on clerical workers, Marshall (1984) on managers, Partington (1976) on teachers and Gamarinkow (1978) on nurses.

4 See, for example, the accounts of Marxist feminists such as Beechey (1978), Bruegel (1982) and Milkman (1976) and those of dual labour market theorists such as Barron and Norris (1976), Edwards *et al.* (1975) and Rubery (1978).

5 See also Allen and Leonard (1976), who suggest a similar sequence.

6 For analyses of the ways in which biological assumptions were embedded in such accounts, see Friedman (1982) and Leonard (1984).

7 See Walby (1986) for a detailed account of such difficulties.

8 This has been explored by a whole series of writers, some of the most important of which are: Marcuse 1969; Reich 1969; Gagnon and Simon 1973; Mitchell 1975; Plummer 1975; Freud 1977; Jackson 1978; Weeks 1981; Rich 1983; Rose 1983; Sayers 1986; Foucault 1987; MacKinnon 1987; Jeffreys 1990.

9 See early works, such as the chapters in Morgan (1970), Bart (1971), Hamblin (1974), Campbell (1974) and Leonard (1980); see also more recent work, e.g. the chapters in Holly (1989) and Holland *et al.* (1990).

10 The conflation of the material with the economic was not, however, only to be found within early Marxist feminist accounts. It also occurred in later accounts which recognized the operation of autonomous patriarchal relations in the labour market and fore-grounded the control of women's access to waged labour as the key to women's subordination in the labour market (i.e. in Walby's and Hartmann's analyses). These accounts see access to waged labour as key to understanding the sexual division of labour and indeed the formation of gender itself; hence forms of economic control (in particular, the control of access to waged labour) are identified as the material basis of men's power over women.

11 For example, how nurses are cast as mistresses of doctors, and how innuendo and flirting constitute an important part of hospital culture (Bradley 1989: 199).

12 See, for example, the Wages for Housework related English Collective of Prostitutes in the UK (Lopez-Jones, 1988), and the National Task Force on Prostitution in the USA (Coyote/NTFP 1988).

13 DiTomaso (1989) also reports similar findings in relation to women in 'non-traditional jobs' based on her research on harassment and discrimination in three workplaces: a heavy manufacturing firm, a non-manufacturing firm and a public organization.

3

Family production in the labour market

In Chapter 2 we saw how, in a number of analyses of the gendering of the labour market, sexuality has been constantly marginalized. But some of these same analyses also completely separate out family production – where goods and services are produced within family relations – from production occurring in the context of the labour market. While there is a recognition that women carry out productive work in the home in the form of domestic work, these studies assume that the production of goods and services for the market no longer takes place within the context of family relations. This derives from a particular analysis of the impact of the development of capitalism upon patriarchal relations.

This history is made explicit by Hartmann (1979), who argues that with the development of capitalism, the social location of production for the market shifted (although at an uneven pace) from the family workshop to production organized on a wider scale, for example in factories: 'Capitalists began to organize production on a larger scale, and production became separated from the home' (Hartmann 1979: 215). In factories, the relations of production were then no longer familial.

The advent of capitalism is thus seen to have not only shifted the location of production for the market, but also to have shifted the major site of the control of women's labour. Prior to the growth of capitalism, patriarchal control of women's (and children's) labour is held to have taken place primarily within the family. But with the development of capitalism, and the separation of market production from the family, this system gave way to new forms of control. These are seen to have developed in response to the threat that the development of capitalist waged employment posed to men's power over women. Waged work potentially offered women escape from economic dependency upon men, and hence threatened the basis of men's control over women.

In response, men organized within the labour market, using similar strategies and techniques of hierarchical organization to those they had previously employed to control women directly within the family. These new forms of control of women's labour ensured men continued to benefit: 'a direct system of control was translated into an indirect, impersonal system of control, mediated by society-wide institutions' (Hartmann 1979: 207). As stressed in Chapter 2, these accounts stress the importance of limitations on women's access to waged labour. They hold the advent of capitalism to have unilaterally shifted the primary site of control of women's labour, but by ensuring women's economic dependency upon men, to have maintained a material basis of patriarchy in both the family and the labour market.

This historical account of the impact of capitalism on patriarchal relations has a number of implications for the relationship between the labour market and family production. First, it assumes that the development of capitalism separated and differentiated non-market and market production, that all production for exchange on the market was moved from the family to the capitalist system. The family thus came to be a site where only non-market production takes place (that is to say, the only goods and services produced within the family are those for household self-consumption and not intended for sale on the market). Conversely, the labour market is defined as a domain in which all production occurs within the nexus of capital–labour relations. It assumes that the only form of work which takes place within the labour market is waged work.

Second, by assuming that production for the market shifts from the family to the capitalist mode within a capitalist demand economy, this account equally assumes that the familial mode of control of women's labour takes place only in relation to non-market production, this being the only form of production recognized to exist within the family household (within 'the domestic mode of production', according to Walby following Delphy). In the labour market, by contrast, the only form of control of women's labour is related to access to wages. In other words, in this account, both the forms of production and the forms of the control of women's labour are fixed in relation to specific social sites; and men's exploitation of women's unpaid labour in the family is the outcome of patriarchal relations operating within the labour market.

Historical analyses have shown, however, that in the process of development of industrial capitalism, many industries had seen a period when family production, and the familial mode of control of labour, operated *within* the structure of capitalist enterprises; when husbands, wives and children all worked for an employer, but only the husbands received a wage.[1] This is generally treated as a strictly historically specific phenomenon which occurred within newly industrializing sectors. It is posited to have disappeared (albeit after a struggle, see Mark-Lawson and Witz 1986) with increased capitalization. It was a historically specific form of labour organization, and also therefore a historically specific mode of control of women's labour for market production. In locating family production in this way, an evolutionary model of market production is implicitly laid down.[2]

A similar evolutionary flavour is also found in much of the literature on petty commodity production (small businesses and self-employment), within which the use of unpaid family labour is typical. Here, despite an acknowledgement of the persistence of this form of production alongside, and indeed as part of, the capitalist formation,[3] it is none the less often referred to as 'pre-capitalist'.[4] Modern, 'fully developed' capitalist enterprises are deemed not to include the family as part of their productive structure.

Thus, although these accounts see both the familial mode of production and production within the family for exchange as operating in the labour market, they stress these were phenomena which disappeared, or in the case of petty commodity production, became very marginal as a result of the logic of capitalist development. They therefore do not disturb the consensus that family production and the direct control and exploitation of women's labour by husbands does not occur within modern capitalist industries.

Research on race and the contemporary labour market has begun to problematize the use of this kind of evolutionary model in relation to the development of market production however, and in relation to the control of women's labour. Phizacklea (1990; see also Phizacklea 1988b), for example, in a study of the fashion industry, has shown that the incidence of family production is linked to the existence of racist relations within the labour market. This bears little if any relation to the logic and stage of capitalist development. She shows, for example, that small firms within the industry are overwhelmingly dominated by male ethnic 'entrepreneurs', that production within these firms (in the form of homeworking) is organized by family hierarchies, and that access to family labour is central for the establishment of these firms. Importantly, Phizacklea also reveals that this form of production is becoming increasingly significant as a productive mode for the industry: '...far from homeworking being an inefficient and uneconomic relic of the productive past, it is actually on the increase in the UK' (Phizacklea 1990: 1–2). She thus actively challenges the assumption found in the 'evolutionary' model of industrial development that the existence of family production is causally and solely linked to the logic of capitalism.[5]

While Phizacklea challenges the notion that family production forms only part of the heritage of industrial production, both Crompton (1986) and Finch (1983) have uncovered the ways in which the unpaid labour of women is directly incorporated into labour market production via wives carrying out unpaid work which is necessary for their husbands' occupations. While neither fully develops the theoretical implications of their research for the gendering of the labour market, their work does problematize the assumption that unpaid production does not contribute to and/or is quite unconnected to labour market production (which is contained in the assertion that capitalist development moved production for the market away from the family). Their research clearly raises questions about the assumption that the only work carried out 'in the context of capitalism' is waged work, and the assumption that the familial mode of control of women's labour only operates in relation to production which is not intended for the market. They show that it is husbands who have access to and who make use of the unpaid work of wives for their paid employment and how their employers benefit whether they be managers, politicians or servicemen. Delphy and Leonard (1992) develop this by looking at the way self-employed businessmen use their wives' unpaid work in their occupations.[6]

In terms of the relationship between family production and the labour market, however, it is clear from the existing literature and research that one of the issues which requires attention is the extent to which production for exchange is or is not related to unpaid family production, and is or is not related to the direct control of women's labour by husbands.

These were the issues I sought to address throughout the study of the hotel and catering section of the British tourist industry, which was described in Chapter 1.

Family labour in hotels and pubs

One of the most distinctive features of the hotel and catering section of the British tourist industry is that its capital structure is overwhelmingly dominated by small, decentralized, relatively autonomous units (Goffee and Scase 1983; HCITB 1985; Bagguley 1987; Urry 1990). Operations in the sector fall into essentially only two categories: large, usually multinational companies which own chains of establishments, and small, owner-proprietor establishments (see Dronfield and Soto, 1982). It is these owner-proprietor establishments (small hotels, guesthouses, bed and breakfast establishments, restaurants, cafes and pubs) which predominate. Existing data suggest that around 80 per cent of all hotel and catering establishments in Britain are small operations in terms of the numbers employed (see, e.g. Dronfield and Soto 1982; and data presented in Bagguley 1987).

While there has been relatively little research on work relations in these small units, what does exist has shown the extent to which these small establishments, like other small businesses, rely upon the unpaid labour of family members for production.[7] Indeed, having access to a 'free' source of labour power is crucial for both their establishment and 'success' (Scase and Goffee 1980a, 1980b). Within small businesses, it is notoriously difficult to achieve economies of scale, and labour costs form a particularly high proportion of total costs. In addition, all service industries are particularly labour-intensive (see Urry 1986, 1990), so their labour costs are proportionately higher. When these two factors are compounded within small service businesses, such as hotel and catering establishments, labour costs are of vital importance in determining whether or not a business 'fails' or 'succeeds'. Without access to an unpaid source of labour in the form of family labour, many small hotel and catering establishments simply could not afford to exist.

Much of the technical literature relating to the hotel and catering sector (HCITB 1985; Smith 1986), and some analyses of the sector (Bagguley 1987; Urry 1990), recognize how extensively family labour is used in small establishments, and how characteristic family production is of such establishments. But they assume that family production does not occur within the sector's large capital operations (just as similar assumptions were made in the generalized, theoretical accounts of family production and its relationship to 'developed capital' discussed earlier). Family production is, in other words, assumed only to operate in small, owner-proprietor hotel and catering establishments – that is, in petit bourgeoise situations, outside the context of the wage-labour structure (see Dronfield and Soto 1982; Goffee and Scase; 1983; HCITB 1985; Bagguley 1987; Urry 1990).

My own research revealed, however, that family production is not confined to small capital operations within the sector. It extends into, and is located within, large capital operations. The unpaid labour of wives is used by men waged workers employed by hotel and catering companies, not only for domestic work but also for occupational work. Furthermore, the location of family production within the wage-labour structure is mediated by labour market mechanisms, that is by mechanisms internal to the labour market itself. It is mediated by contractual agreements between men waged workers who are employed as establishment managers within the hotel and catering sector and their (often multinational corporation) employers. A variety of types of companies use these agreements, and find the family production involved highly advantageous.

This raises important challenges not only to analyses of the hotel and catering sector, but also to existing analyses of the relationship between family production and market production. Perhaps even more significantly, it raises problems about existing analyses of the internal dynamics of the labour market, in particular analyses of the forms of control of women's labour operating within the labour market. Before turning to these theoretical discussions, however, the evidence for the existence and importance of family production within the hotel and catering sector needs to be presented. The data derive from a series of interviews with people representing different interest groups in relation to the use of family labour in hotel and catering establishments, namely men managers of hotel and catering establishments, wives of managers, representatives of various hotel and catering companies (in particular, personnel managers working at the headquarters of hotel and catering companies), and representatives from occupational associations. Information has also been drawn from hotel and catering trade journals.

Family production in the waged-labour context

A substantial number of large companies which own chains of hotels, restaurants and pubs, use married couples to manage their establishments. Until relatively recently, the largest international hotel company operating within Britain, which owns several different chains of hotels here and abroad, operated policies whereby not only did all managers have to be men, but it was also compulsory that the men employed were married, and that their wives were available to work in the hotels as part of a married management 'team'. While this particular company has recently changed the requirement that all managers be married, it nevertheless still insists that particular types of hotels require married managers. The company prefers, for example, to employ married couples to manage hotels which are used primarily by tourists.

This employment practice is common in many large companies in the hotel and catering sector. It is, however, even more evident in relation to the public house section of the sector. The five largest brewery companies currently operating in the UK, which between them own the majority of Britain's pubs, rely extensively upon married management teams to run these outlets. For example, one company insists that all of its managers are men and that they are married (indeed, at one stage, this company required potential pub managers to produce marriage certificates during job interviews); 80 per cent of the pubs of another company are managed by married couples.

A glance at the appointments section of any of the hotel and catering trade journals confirms the significance of married management teams for the sector. Advertisements for general management positions in hotels and pubs (across operations of various capital sizes) specify that married couples are required in 50 and 75 per cent of cases, respectively. Examples include 'Manager with Spouse to Assist', 'Live-In-Management Couple Required for 29 Bedroom Hotel' and 'Several Couples Required for Pub Management'.

When hotel and catering companies use married couples to run establishments in this way, the employment contracts used specify that both husbands and wives are required to work in the establishments. But despite wives being formally included in the contract, the employment contract itself – that is, the wage-labour contract – operates only between husbands and the company. Only the husband receives wages: the monthly pay cheque is made out to him alone. Thus although the labour of wives is included in the contract, it is assumed to constitute part of husbands' labour by the hotel and catering companies. Companies buy the labour power of wives *through* their husbands, paying about one and a quarter times as much to a married team as to the (rare) single man manager. The management work done by wives is directly controlled and appropriated by their husbands, who exchange their own labour power and that of wives with the companies. Women working in married management 'teams', who produce goods and services within hotel and catering establishments for sale on the market, therefore work in conditions of direct appropriation of their labour by husbands. In these circumstances, wives are dependent for their maintenance on the 'boss' in return for their domestic work and their work in the hotel, restaurant or bar. In the case of management teams, the form of wage-labour agreement operating between husbands and employers thus acts as a mechanism to 'facilitate' family production within hotel and catering establishments and both husbands and companies abstract considerable benefits from it.

Hotel and catering companies and the 'employment' of married management 'teams'

From the point of view of the hotel and catering companies which employ married teams, using couples to manage their establishments has considerable advantages. The one most commonly cited by company representatives concerns the labour which can be extracted. Many companies who use married teams (particularly breweries) do so because single men managers (this being assumed to be the only possible alternative to married management teams) would simply not be able to cope with managing and running establishments on their own. This is not because the companies think the amount of work required to manage many of their establishments is necessarily too much for one person, but rather because single men will not put in enough work for the establishments to be run successfully. The companies' solution is simple: employ married couples, not because husbands and wives will share the work, each doing equal amounts, but rather because (it is believed) wives will do a disproportionate amount of the work. As one brewery company personnel manager said: 'We have to get someone to do the work, so we buy the wives in'. This 'buying in' of wives is achieved through an employment contract with the woman's husband. He is appointed an establishment manager, on the condition his wife works there.

A second benefit cited by companies, and one which is also labour-related, is the greater reliability of married teams. This quality is unequivocally seen to be provided by wives. The companies argue that they cannot rely on men on their own to run their establishments successfully. In particular, they suggest, men cannot be relied upon to carry out many of the essential, routine, difficult and 'hidden' (particularly administrative) tasks. One company's personnel manager gave book-keeping as an example. He said men simply could not be relied upon to do the books. Either they forgot to do them, or if they did remember, they did them illegibly or incorrectly. This created huge problems for the company's accountants. But, he went on, when married couples manage establishments, wives not only consistently remember to do the books, but also do them legibly and correctly. Wives, unlike their husbands, are therefore reliable workers. In particular, companies can rely upon wives to carry out many of the hidden tasks, such as making up wages, PAYE and VAT returns, chasing up unpaid invoices, and contracting cleaners, which are all essential to the successful running of their establishments.

Another central benefit of using married management teams for hotel and catering companies, and the one forming the central logic behind their use, particularly by brewery companies with chains of pubs, is that a married couple increases a particular type of custom. Companies argue that establishments managed by married couples are generally more successful in terms of sales than those run by single men. This again is a phenomenon seen to derive from the presence of wives within the establishment. Put simply, companies regard wives as 'sexual attractions' who will boost sales. Wives being present encourages men customers to use the establishments. According to a personnel manager in one of the large brewery companies, 'Lots of blokes come into our pubs to drink because of the wives. They [men] like being served by women . . . We [the company] like using married couples because of the custom that wives generate'. This company believes this premise is borne out by its figures – the same personnel manager went on to affirm that the pubs managed by married couples have higher sales than pubs run by single men.

A further advantage cited systematically by companies using married management teams is that this practice cuts wage costs. The total wages bill for management of many establishments, especially hotels where several managers are required, can be substantially reduced by using married management teams. One of the major hotel companies, for example, estimates that the total cost of wages for married management teams is approximately 75 per cent of that which would be required if its establishments were run by single persons. A personnel manager at the national headquarters of the company explained quite directly that husband and wife management teams were used so the company could pay a 'lesser sum' than if it employed extra managers. This cheapness is seen as essentially deriving from wives. The labour of wives is regarded as 'bought in' when the companies employ husbands, so it is the wives' labour that is regarded as cheap – it costs only 25 per cent of that of husbands.

In sum, the use of married management teams is seen directly as highly advantageous for the hotel and catering companies. They reduce labour costs (particularly in establishments where several managers would normally be required), increase sales, ensure a reliable and disciplined workforce, and their use leads to the successful running and management of establishments.

What is most striking is that all these advantages are benefits deriving from using the work of wives. Whether it be their reliability or their capacity to increase sales, wives in teams provide the hotel and catering companies with essential services which ensure the success of their establishments. But despite the centrality of women to the running of the establishments, and the disproportionate amounts of work they do compared with their husbands, women are neither directly employed as managers in their own right, nor when married do they receive anything directly from the company. Companies employ men and pay 'joint' wages directly to husbands.

The work relations of husbands and wives within hotel and catering establishments

Examination of the division of labour between husbands and wives working as married managers, in particular the dynamics of the control of labour within the teams (i.e. who decides who does what and when), reveals the ways in which husbands directly control the labour of their wives. One striking fact predominates: there is no job description for wives in such teams. The tasks wives are to do remains unspecified by the companies. This lack of specificity derives from the companies' assumption that husbands will exercise direct control within establishments, for husbands, in contrast, are specifically given responsibility for managing the labour of all employees, including that of their wives. Thus, despite the formal incorporation of wives into the management contract, companies regard only the husbands as 'the managers'.

When interviewed, the wives of hotel and catering establishment managers confirmed that they were aware that the companies regard only husbands as managers, and also that their husbands did in fact control the division of tasks between them. They explained how they are systematically not recognized as being 'part of the management'. Breweries, for instance, usually put liquor licences in the husband's name only, and when companies have 'serious business' to do, for example discussing potential changes, they go straight to the husbands. Wives also suggested various ways in which husbands exercise control. The wife of a pub manager explained how her husband does the jobs in the pub which he enjoys, and she does those he does not like. She said how when they first began to work in the pub, her husband worked mostly 'on the wet side', that is managing the supply of drinks for the bar, while she served behind the bar and prepared the food which they sold. However, her husband then discovered how he enjoyed cooking, and so he decided he wanted to cook the pub food. He reordered the division of tasks between them – not only according to tasks but also to his moods. He cooked 'when he felt like it', while she had to be flexible (and watchful), varying her work according to the tasks her husband had decided to carry out on a particular day. She also handled all staff matters, including the hiring and firing of bar and cleaning staff. Her husband argued he hated doing this and was useless at it. Claiming a lack of skills in relation to a particular task or tasks is indeed a common method used by husbands to control the work of wives. Another husband, for instance, said that he was not good at the 'business side of things' (including all the bookwork, payment of wages, VAT and PAYE, and ordering food and bar stocks) and that his wife knew she had to do it if it was to get done.

The most typical division of tasks between husbands and wives within management 'teams' is, however, one where the husband 'fronts' the management of establishments, playing 'mine host', greeting customers and wandering around and checking the activities in a hotel, or managing the activities of the bar in a pub; while wives are allocated to, for example, managing the housekeeping section in a hotel or preparing and serving food, or serving behind the bar in a pub. In one hotel, the husband explained the logic of this division of labour as being obvious: wives do work in the hotel which is 'just' an extension of what they do in the home – the housework and caring for people (in this case, his wife also handled all customer queries and complaints). Wives, he argued, are 'more suited' to managing the housekeeping section than husbands. But even when there is this relatively fixed division of tasks, if husbands get bored with what they are doing, they call upon their wives to cover for them. Husbands often want to 'pop out', or 'check up' on something/someone. But this does not happen the other way round. Wives constantly have to drop whatever they are doing to fit in with what their husbands want to do.

Husbands themselves stress a variety of benefits deriving from their wives working in their establishments. In particular, they stress the range of services available to them from their wives, which go far beyond what would be available from a 'regular' employee. For example, one manager said he would always expect, and could rely upon, his wife to work any hours required in the hotel. This he pointed out is not possible with other workers. In addition to the relative limitless nature of his wife's time, this manager also stressed the advantages of the extra sorts of work 'you' can 'expect' from a wife, which again are not available from employees. He specified taking 'extra care' with customers and paying special attention to the appearance of the hotel: putting out flowers and making sure it is extra clean, 'just as if it [the hotel] were her own home'.

As has already been stated, the wives themselves are not paid wages by the companies, rather the 'joint' salary is paid directly to husbands. It is thus up to husbands to decide how much and what wives receive for their work. Wives are therefore dependent upon their boss/head of household for their maintenance. Both husbands and wives when interviewed spoke of the wages as being 'his', some of which he 'gave' to her (although the exact amounts were not disclosed). The 'joint' wages are, in fact, fairly low. In pubs, for instance, they ranged between £11,000 and £15,000 in 1989. But a substantial amount of additional money is made through the bonuses which companies (in particular breweries) operate in relation to sales. Companies set monthly sales targets for each establishment, and if sales are above this target, then managers are entitled to extra money. It is husbands who receive this bonus, which is added on to their monthly wages cheque.

For husbands, the use by companies of management teams means they derive all manner of benefits. Not only do they get the basic benefits of being married (domestic, emotional, and sexual servicing from wives; Delphy and Leonard 1992), they also have control and autonomy in their employment situation. They can do the work they want to do, when they want to do it, and rely on their wives to be flexible to cover for them. They can also rely on their wives to work any hours required, and to carry out good quality work. They appropriate directly all of the wives' occupational work, receiving wages not only for their own work, but also for that of their wives. They thus have direct control over all the household's money.

Events following a merger between a major hotel company (which used a system of married management teams within its establishments) and a company with operations spread more widely across the leisure and tourism industry, show clearly husbands' support for the use of management teams. Shortly after the merger, there was a policy shift in the personnel specifications for hotel managers. Although hotel managers still had to be men, they did not necessarily have to be married. Indeed, from this point onwards the newly formed company specifically preferred not to 'appoint' married teams to manage their hotels. This shift was one outcome of an overall restructuring of the operations of the newly formed company. These were aimed at integrating and central-izing the various operations brought together by the merger (which included hotels, restaurants and catering suppliers). One particular strand of this restructuring was an attempt to unify and systematize labour organization within the various establishments and outlets owned by the company, because the newly formed company wanted both to centralize and to increase control over its workforce.

One of the 'casualties' of this restructuring was the existing personnel policy in relation to managers of hotels. In this general climate of centralization of control, and in particular of attempts to gain increased control over the workforce, the existing manage-ment system was held to give men managers too much control, power and autonomy within individual hotels. By changing the policy on married managers, the company aimed to reduce their autonomy by reducing their power within hotels. In doing so, it hoped to gain increased control over the management and internal organization of establishments.

The response to this shift in policy was telling. The married men managers interviewed told of how they themselves, and others throughout the company, directly opposed the change. This opposition was one mobilized by the losses men general managers as a group within the company would incur in the event of such a restructuring. In particular, they faced a reduction in the amount of control they had over the workforce and over how things were organized and run in their establishments. If this particular hotel company, which owned many large establishments, did remove teams, it would mean that extra management staff would need to be employed to substitute for the work wives had until now performed. General managers would have less control over these other managers than they did over their wives. Further, the restructuring meant that general managers faced a reduction in wages with the removal of their wives' labour from their employment contracts. While the proportion of the 'joint' wages attributed to a wife's labour power exchanged by her husband was in no way equal to that of the man's own, it nevertheless constituted a substantial part of the total income. Managers as a group, therefore, faced a 25 per cent cut in wages if the restructuring went ahead.

One manager working for the company said the change in policy was 'the biggest mistake that [the hotel company] ever made', because it meant losing the 'best' and 'most efficient' way of running hotels. However, such 'efficiency' is dependent upon the systematic exploitation of the labour of wives, and it is 'best' for both husbands and companies only because they benefit from it.

Despite the opposition from managers to this restructuring of personnel policy, there was no organized resistance. There were no existing effective forms of worker organization through which such opposition could be channelled, and hotel managers were not represented at the level of policy formation. Rather, opposition tended to take the form of individual action. Most commonly, managers lodged verbal complaints with regional personnel managers, who in general were sympathetic to their cause. In turn, regional managers 'passed on' the complaints of managers to national headquarters. But despite the dissatisfaction levelled at the policy changes by hotel managers, and the clear unpopularity of the measures with employees, the company was determined to carry through the restructuring it deemed necessary after the merger, even though it would increase wage-labour costs. Indeed, at the time there was a general climate of hostility towards hotel managers on the part of the company. The company believed the managers had had too good a deal for too long, and that they expected their powers in relation to the company to parallel those they had in the hotels they managed. The opposition managers were showing was precisely the kind of action the company planned to circumvent through its restructuring. Such opposition, therefore, apparently made the company even more determined to carry through its planned measures.

The opposition to these changes by managers was thus ineffectual. The company went ahead with its restructuring, and from then on it was no longer obligatory for managers to be married.

But the policy change did not mean a simple removal of teams from the company, for those who had been appointed before the changes kept their contracts, and they continued to work in hotels as married management teams.

However, despite the management policy restructuring, this hotel company is now once again actively recruiting married teams for many of its hotels. (Indeed, that they ever stopped doing so is viewed as rather unorthodox within the trade.) This U-turn in policy is part of an attempt to raise standards within the company's hotels. This increase in standards is yet another instance of the benefits to be gained by hotel companies through the exploitation of the work of wives via their formal incorporation into the running of hotels. The hotel manager quoted above said of the U-turn, '[the hotel company] have realized that married couples make the best managers of their hotels, and is the way to keep standards high'.

All of the evidence presented so far − that women working within these management teams receive no wages, that their duties are not specified by the companies, that husbands control the division of labour directly, and that wives' work in hotels and pubs is open-ended − shows the conditions under which wives within these teams work. Despite being referred to as part of management teams by the companies who use them, wives have no labour contract. They do not work in the establishments as employees, but rather they work directly for their husbands. Women in management teams work within hotel and catering establishments as wives. They work there because they are married to managers who are employees. The contract under which the wives work is the marriage contract, not an employment contract, except in so far as the marriage contract is an employment contract (Delphy 1970, 1984). Within this framework, the control that husbands exert over their wives (that is, the control of the labour of wives), and the benefits that husbands extract, derive directly from the patriarchal structuring of the family.

Although the wives are aware of some of the shortcomings of their work situation, they level any dissatisfaction they have at the hotel and catering companies, not at their husbands. Wives in pubs, for instance, complained of the company's practice of putting the liquor trading licences in the name of the husband. But those who were interviewed said they found their work interesting, especially compared with jobs they had had previously, which typically included clerical and secretarial work. That is, working in a pub or hotel offered these women more interesting and enjoyable work than available employment.

Hotel and catering companies make use of these restricted employment opportunities for women, and of family relations, to exploit wives and, as has been shown, to derive their own benefits from these sets of relations. These benefits are achieved by formally incorporating wives' labour into husbands' wage-labour contracts. In so doing, companies gain access into patriarchal family hierarchies, within which husbands appropriate and direct wives' labour. By 'tapping into' family hierarchies in this way, companies derive many advantages from men's control of women's work in family relationships. The payment of wages only to husbands, and the control of wives' labour conferred onto husbands by the labour contract, reinforces and compounds marital relations. It ensures for the company (and for husbands) that wives in these teams remain dependent upon their husbands. It also acts as a mechanism for ensuring that the relations of production – whereby hotel and catering goods and services for the market are produced within family relations – continue within the company's establishments. This in turn provides the profits which allow companies to continue to derive the advantages available to them through their use of management teams, and hence to continue to exploit wives' labour.

Hotel and catering companies' extensive reliance upon this system of management within their establishments, and husbands' direct appropriation, control and exploitation of the labour of wives, shows clearly that both family production and the familial mode of control and exploitation of women's labour are actively operating *within* the contemporary labour market. That such relations of production are to be found located and firmly established within the contemporary 'developed' capitalist labour market is of great theoretical importance, for it challenges directly many of the analyses of employment relations discussed so far in this book. First, it challenges assumptions about the relationship between family production and the large capital section of the hotel and catering sector within the existing literature on work relations in the tourist industry. Second, it further problematizes existing accounts of the relationship between family production and production for exchange. And, finally, it challenges analyses of forms of control of women's labour operating within the contemporary labour market (outlined in Chapter 2). The exact nature of each of these challenges is addressed in the following section.

The implications of family production in the waged-labour context

Earlier in this chapter, it was shown that although there has been some recognition of the importance of family production within small hotel and catering establishments, this form of production has been assumed not to be present within the sector's large capital operations. Implicit in these accounts is the general assumption that family production is simply and unproblematically related to degrees of capitalization within a sector: family production is assumed only to occur in the owner-proprietor (i.e. the self-employed) segment, and not to operate within 'developed' sections of capital.[8] These accounts thus implicitly assume that as soon as self-employed men can afford to do so, they will stop using family labour; that as soon as there is wage labour, there is no family labour. Family labour and wage labour are, in other words, assumed to be mutually exclusive.

These assumptions about family production were also shown to be prevalent in general, cross-sector, accounts of the labour market and in historical work on the use of family production within particular industries. Family production is taken to be a *transitory* labour structure in industrial development: a stage in the 'evolution' of capitalism. It has been assumed not to occur in what would be considered to be 'developed' sections of capital, including the large capital portion of the hotel and catering sector. This 'evolutionary' model of the development of market production in fact underpins the accounts of market production within the hotel and catering sector. The equation of family production with small capital and self-employment assumes that increased capitalization transfers all production for exchange away from the family, and that family production is confined to those sections of capital considered to be relatively underdeveloped, or to newly established (including immigrant-run) companies.

But rather than there being a simple relationship between family production and small capital/self-employment, and its being restricted to a stage in the development of capital or individual companies, the evidence presented in this chapter has shown that family production is firmly established in sections of industrial sectors which are 'fully developed'. It can operate as a productive mode within a waged portion of a sector and be used by companies which operate within national and global economies.

That family production clearly does exist *within* the labour market also challenges the analyses of the gendered operations of the labour market discussed in Chapter 2, which assume that the development of industrial capitalism shifted the production of goods and services for exchange from the family to the labour market and that with this shift came a change in the location and form of control of women's labour – from direct control by individual men in the family, to indirect control based on the restriction of women's access to wages by men more generally in the labour market.

First, the assumption that the development of industrial capitalism separated the family from the production of goods and services for exchange and moved all such production into the labour market has to be questioned. It has already been problematized by researchers who have pointed out that goods and services for exchange are still produced in the family mode of production in various sectors where people are often self-employed – among, for example, small farmers, shopkeepers and newly established businesses.[9] In addition, Finch (1983) has identified many employed men's jobs which draw on the labour of wives, especially where the men work at or from home. Furthermore, much paid employment and self-employment for women is based *in* the home (e.g. Davidoff 1979; Allen and Walkowitz 1987). But none of these studies has identified what was found in hotel and catering management: production within the family mode taking place in a public arena for wages within multinational companies.

What is so striking about this sector of tourism is that employers are so direct about the use of wives' labour, and that the 'team's' place of employment and home are one and the same place – and that this public workplace/private home belongs to the company they work for. Management teams are expected to live in accommodation provided on site – they need special permission to do otherwise – and the value of the accommodation is deemed to be one of the reasons for their low wages.

This study therefore adds weight to the questions raised by earlier work about the extent to which there has actually been a separation of production for the market from family relations. The family production which occurs in this occupation is physically and analytically located as part of the labour market, placed and secured there by labour market mechanisms, by the labour contract which operates between husbands and employers. However, it is also placed and secured there by familial mechanisms, by the marital contract which operates between husbands and wives.

This throws into relief the problems with the spatial metaphor (and cultural assumption) which is embedded in talking about family production as 'outside of', and articulating with, the labour market. 'The family' and 'the labour market' are not separate 'sites', but mutually constructed, even if there has been a lot of cultural effort devoted over the last 150 years to keeping them conceptually distinct and geographically separate (Davidoff 1976; Davidoff *et al.* 1976).

Second, and deriving from this, the analysis of changes in the location and form of control of women's labour proposed by Hartmann and Walby is also problematic. They suggest there has been a shift in the major site of control of women's labour from the family to the labour market, and a change from family patriarchy to capitalist patriarchal control – from direct control by individual men in the family, to indirect control, based on the restriction of women's access to wages, by men more generally in the labour market. [This is part of what Walby (1990) describes as a general shift from private to public patriarchy.]

That family production is so embedded within the labour market in hotel and catering makes us question these assumptions – as well as their model of 'the family' and 'the labour market' as two spatially and conceptually distinct 'sites'. In hotel and catering management, women's labour for exchange is controlled within a non-capitalist mode. That is to say, work done in a public place, which produces goods and services for exchange, is exploited in a system of direct, familial control, rather than by the indirect, exclusionary control they assume to be characteristic of the public sphere.

Both Hartmann and Walby fix and separate out family and

market production within capitalist society. Hartmann sees the family as a non-capitalist mode of control of women's labour, articulating with market control (see Hartmann 1979), whereas Walby sees it as a mode of production of goods and services not intended for exchange, that is domestic production for household consumption (see Walby 1986, 1990). They designate family production as either 'pre'-capitalist (in the case of production for exchange), or limited to production for self-consumption (in domestic production). They argue that while family production was once dominant, the two sites are now either balanced but potentially in competition for women's labour (Hartmann), or that it is now the labour market (i.e. women's position within it and their low wages) which is the main cause of their oppression, and their continued dependence on men (Walby).

Either way, like much feminist research on women's 'work', their focus is pre-eminently on women's relation to waged work – to capital-labour contracts within the labour market – and they assume not only that family work is separate from labour market work, but also that the only form of work to take place 'within' the labour market is waged work. However, as we have seen, family work can be part of labour market work, and the work of women/wives is then unpaid.

Recent research on family production within occupations other than tourism supports the suggestion that such family production is of considerable importance. Finch (1983) showed just how many occupations – from heads of state and ambassadors through politicians, managers of multinational companies, soldiers, architects and vicars, to insurance salesman and gasmen 'on call' – need a wife if they are to be satisfactorily performed. In addition, she demonstrates various ways in which employers elicit unpaid work from the wives of their employees. Most such unpaid occupational/labour market work done by wives goes quite unrecognized because of the pervasive assumption that production for exchange within the public sphere is always accompanied by a wage. Family production operating within the labour market, therefore, undoubtedly extends far beyond the hotel and catering sector.

A further outcome of analyses seeing the economic dimensions of women's oppression only in terms of waged labour relations is that the actual forms of work women carry out in the labour market receive very little attention. This has lead not only to an *a priori* exclusion of the possibility of women doing unpaid work for the labour market, but also to the exclusion of forms of women's 'work' which are not part of what is commonly recognized as industrial waged labour.

The next section will once again draw on the work of wives in management teams to show that what is assumed to constitute 'work' within accounts such as those of Hartmann and Walby is problematic. The empirical material reveals forms of work carried out by wives which are exploited and appropriated by both husbands and capital, but which fall outside the normally used category of work or labour, and which have also been excluded from feminist analyses of the labour market.

Forms of work and women's labour in the case of married management 'teams'

The use of family production in the hotel and catering sector reaps a number of benefits for husbands and for capital, and this work takes a whole variety of different forms. As was noted, the labour of wives has particular advantageous qualities, and the work they do which gets appropriated is not just the labour they expend on the production of the more obvious goods and services for 'their' establishment, but includes other, additional forms of labour.

Wives' labour is efficient and reliable, it is on call 24 hours a day and it cuts the wages bill. Wives also help to increase sales in establishments and keep their husbands healthy and hardworking. The first three aspects of wives' labour relate straightforwardly to what would usually be considered as the 'work' involved in the production of goods and services for exchange, for example the production of food for sale in pubs, the cleaning of hotels, and so on. Such work clearly constitutes a substantial part of the labour of wives which is exploited by their use in management teams. But what is also clear, is that other, different forms of work – sexual work and caring work – also constitutes part of wives' exploited labour, since the fourth advantage for the hotel and catering companies noted above, the increase in sales, comes about by virtue of wives being 'sexual attractions', and the fifth because wives do 'emotional', 'health' and other caring work for their husbands, looking after them mentally and physically (making sure they eat properly, stopping them working too hard and 'keeping them off the booze').[10]

Wives constitute 'custom pullers' for their husbands and for their husbands' employers because of their 'attractiveness' and social interactional skills. As one brewery personnel manager said: 'Lots of blokes come into our pubs to drink because of the wives. They [men] like being served by women . . . we [the company] like using married couples because of the custom the wives generate'. Note that it is not wives in and of themselves that constitute sexual attractions, but rather that their 'sexual attractiveness' is somehow embodied into the work they do: men 'like being served by women'. This implies that part of the work of serving drinks behind a bar for wives involves a sexual element, that there is some kind of sexual 'exchange' between wives and men customers. Because the companies are gaining benefits from this 'sexual work' in the form of increased sales, some of which is returned to husbands in bonuses, this work is being exploited and appropriated by the companies and by husbands. Thus, wives working within management teams carry out forms of sexual work as part of their unpaid family work.

Given that 'sexual' labour is part of the work being carried out by wives in the context of management teams, and that this form of labour is appropriated by husbands and employers, it can be seen that the exploitation of women's labour within the labour market includes not only the unpaid production of goods and services, but also the exploitation of a form of work which extends well beyond what is usually considered to be 'productive activity' within labour market theory (Adkins and Lury 1992).

In Chapter 2, the issue was raised that in most labour market analyses sexuality is not recognized as having any economic value: it is not seen to have an economic dimension, nor to constitute a form of productive work. Even the few theorists concerned with the gendered dynamics of the labour market who have to some extent discussed the significance of 'sexuality' (e.g. Pringle 1989a, 1989b; Cockburn 1991) do not recognize the possibility that labour market work may in part be constituted by sexual work, or that forms of sexual work may be routinely carried out by women (paid or unpaid) in the labour market.

That women working within management 'teams' appear to be carrying out just such sexual work therefore raises important questions for an understanding of both the dynamics of the control and exploitation of women's labour within the labour market, and consequently for understanding the gendering of the labour market. These questions include the relative significance of sexual work in the construction of women's general position in the labour market (for instance, in what ways women as workers are controlled through these forms of labour). Also, the extent to which women workers as a group perform this 'extra' form of work, and where they perform it, and how and why.

The following chapter will use evidence from studies of two worksites (the leisure park and hotel) to consider both the significance and extent of the sexual work identified in this chapter in possibly structuring 'women's work' in the labour market generally.

Notes

1 See, for example, Smelser (1959), Anderson (1971) and Savage (1982) on the cotton industry and Mark-Lawson and Witz (1986) on the coal mining industry, both in the nineteenth century.

2 The use of such an evolutionary model is fairly commonplace. Clark (1982), for example, assumes that family production is a transitory form of production which was operative in the shift from feudalism to capitalism, but which is no longer important as a productive mode in 'developed' capitalist industries (see also Minge 1986).

3 See Newby *et al.* (1981) on farmers and Bechhofer and Elliot (1981) on small shopkeepers.

4 See, for example, Bertaux and Bertaux-Wiame (1981) on bakers in France.

5 For similar critiques of the evolutionary model, see the chapters in Westwood and Bhachu (1988), Mies (1986) and Cockburn (1991).

6 Indeed, men's appropriation of their wives' labour in their occupational work is increasingly being recognized as being of significance to a variety of social formations, including international politics (Enloe 1989), corporate identities (Kanter 1977; Callan and Ardener 1984), national and ethnic identities (Yuval-Davis and Anthias 1989; Enloe 1989) and colonialism and imperialism (Callan and Ardner 1984; Ware 1992).

7 See Scase and Goffee (1980a, 1980b) for general accounts of the centrality of family labour for small businesses, and see Goffee and Scase (1983) and Bagguley (1987) for this sector in particular.

8 For example, Goffee and Scase (1983) and Bagguley (1987) assume this relationship in their analyses of the capital structure of the sector.
9 See, for example, Delphy (1970) on farming and the various occupations looked at by Bechhofer and Elliot (1981), Westwood and Bhachu (1988) and Scase and Goffee (1980a, 1980b).
10 This is an important area of wives' work, but one which requires another book if it is to be explored in detail.

4

Sexual servicing and women's employment

The other part of my work on tourism looked at the gendered structure and the dynamics of work in two tourist organizations – a hotel and a leisure park – in order to explore the relationship between sexuality and the gendered organization of employment relations.[1] The fieldwork itself took place over a 6 month period, from April to September 1989. Numerous visits to the two establishments were made and my activities ranged from watching and listening, to carrying out a series of in-depth interviews and attending staff training sessions. I also collected a range of documentary evidence from personnel records and various in-house and company-wide publications. The interviewees included general managers of the establishments, various departmental managers (sometimes up to three or four interviews with just one individual) and women and men workers. In addition, a series of interviews were held with various representatives from the parent companies of both the leisure park and the hotel.

As I became better known at the workplaces, I found myself involved in many informal discussions with employees, who often provided valuable insights into particular aspects of the operation of the establishments. Crucially, this meant that many of the women employees I interviewed fairly early on during the fieldwork began to report on a regular basis particular incidents in relation to their own employment experiences and those of other women workers. This was particularly the case at the leisure park, where the degree of access granted was far greater than that for the hotel. As a result, the body of data collected from the leisure park was both wide-ranging and rich, whereas that from the hotel (which consists mostly of management interviews, written sources and observation) seems modest by comparison. Even this was gained with some difficulty. It was not, for example, possible to photocopy any of the written sources (it all had to be copied by hand). Fortunately, however, the two data sets complemented each other. Since confidentiality was assured during the fieldwork, in what follows the hotel will be referred to by the pseudonym 'Global Hotel' and the leisure park by 'Fun Land'.

Service labour: 'people' work

My first contact with any personnel from these tourist operations took the form of interviews with their general managers. While discussion in these interviews was wide-ranging (including, for example, how both operations were organized and functioned, their employment practices and their customer profiles), what was outstanding was that both general managers gave strikingly similar accounts of the characteristics of 'work' in their respective establishments. Indeed, this account came up time and time again during the fieldwork – it was found, for instance, in various workplace publications such as employee rule books, and similar ones were given by various middle managers and by representatives from the parent companies.

In this account of 'work', the success of both Fun Land and Global Hotel was seen to be primarily related to, and dependent upon, the 'quality' of their employees, and in particular the quality of those employees who have direct contact with customers. At Global Hotel, for example, the personnel manager argued simply that 'the hotel is the staff'. Any other factors which could be seen to be related or contribute to its success (such as its swimming pool, gym, riverside location, restaurant or conference suite) were completely ruled out. Similarly, the personnel and training manager at Fun Land suggested that its success 'does not depend upon the physical amenities on offer to customers [for example, the rides, the bars and the catering facilities], but rather depends upon the type of employees ... the only difference between different amusement parks is the employees'.

The 'quality' or 'type' of employees to whom the representatives of Global Hotel and Fun Land were referring were those who were seen to have the abilities and skills to interact and 'handle' customers in what was considered to be an appropriate manner. This involved using what both the personnel and the training managers described as 'people' skills. The training manager working with the staff at Fun Land explained: 'the jobs we are offering to people are very important because the workers "out there" [working directly with customers] are the one's who bring the money in . . . because of this we have to ask them to develop people skills'. Here, a direct connection is being made between the production of profit and workers' deployment of these 'people' skills in their interactions with customers.

Similarly, Fun Land's employee handbook states:

> Fun Land's . . . aim is to provide fun and pleasure for the people who visit us . . . and our visitors return again and again. They do so because the Staff at [Fun Land] have regarded these visitors as guests. You greet them when they arrive. You help them on and off the devices. You serve them with food and drink. You entertain them. You serve them in the shops. You keep the Amusement Park clean and tidy for them. But more than that, only You can provide the friendly atmosphere which will promote the continuing success of the Company. [Fun Land] is here to enable people to enjoy their leisure time, to bring gaiety to their holidays and to above all make them smile. Certainly [Fun Land] is a money making operation, but no operation is successful if the customer is not satisfied with the product. To this extent You are a most important part of this Company, for You are a vital part of the product. Our visitors come here to enjoy the happy environment which You help to create. Remember, it is your work to make others happy.

Here, once again, a clear connection is being made between the forms of employee interaction with customers and Fun Land's success, to the extent that employees themselves are located as part of the product. But, in addition, this excerpt substantiates the meaning of the 'people' skills desired of workers. These are revealed to include satisfying customers, caring for them as if they were guests, making them feel happy and making them smile. Ultimately, this excerpt suggests, the use and operationalization of these skills by workers in relation to customers is more important than any of the other goods and services that Fun Land can provide. 'People' skills, and the work involved in them, is thus designated a far greater significance than the 'physical' operations of, for example, cleaning the park, working the rides or preparing food.

In a similar vein, part of Global Hotel's workers' handbook reads:

> Our business is caring for guests, they are the reason for our being, we look to them for our lead. Anyone who comes in contact with our hotel is a guest. Guests can take many forms and each has their own respective needs. The reason that guests choose this hotel are as many and varied as the guests themselves but, above all, what makes them elect to stay with us is the warmth and friendliness and the highest standard of service and efficiency. Your role as part of the Team, is to make our guests welcome, happy and comfortable. You are an ambassador for our hotel and also for the company and are best placed to provide the warmest welcome and best service. You are the eyes and ears of our hotel. If you meet guests regularly you can see what they want and hear what they ask for. Your care and attention to detail mean that our guests will return again and again.

Here, again, explicit links are made between workers using their 'people' skills, in the form of being warm and friendly and making guests feel happy and comfortable, and the production of a successful establishment. The mobilization of these skills means that guests will return 'again and again'. People skills are again ascribed a primary status in the production of this success. 'Above all' – that is above all of the other activities workers perform, and above all of the hotel's facilities – it is the friendliness and warmth of staff combined with 'the highest standard of service and efficiency' which produces custom.

The significance attributed to workers performing 'people' work was also in clear view in staff training at the two establishments. During one standard training session at Fun Land, for instance, approximately three-quarters of the time was devoted to them. During this time, the training manager suggested that it was the primary duty of seasonal staff to create 'good' customer relations. To this end, he argued, 'at all times employees must be helpful, caring, courteous and smiling'. If employees failed to provide these services, they would not be fulfilling the role expected of them as staff by Fun Land, and would not, he argued, be doing their jobs properly. The training manager went on to explain that not only did Fun Land expect its employees to carry out these services, but what Fun Land really required was that employees put 'that little bit extra' into their delivery. They should not just be helpful and caring, but 'extra' helpful and 'extra' caring. By providing that 'little bit extra', employees would not only be 'making the customer's day', but also contributing significantly to the success of the company by assuring it has a good reputation and, he argued, encouraging more custom.

But what the training specified was required of the staff in relation to the production of 'good' customer relations was, however, not limited to forms of employee behaviour in relation to customers. Being friendly, helpful and courteous was not enough. The training manager argued it also involved employees having high 'personal standards', particularly in relation to appearance and hygiene. Because 'impressions count' at Fun Land, he stressed that the maintenance of these personal standards were of the utmost importance.

Thus the account of people work (or what was referred to interchangeably as customer relations) given in staff training sessions bore many similarities to that found elsewhere at both workplaces. Indeed, the definition of work was consistent in each case and there were many continuities in the way in which it was constructed within the two worksites. This shared construction of work can be summarized as having three main strands or characteristics. First, the most important form of work within both worksites was constructed as being people work/customer relations. This work was systematically designated a status above and beyond any other forms of work carried out by employees, such as the 'physical' activities of stocking the catering kiosks, serving drinks or mowing the grass. Second, the meaning of this form of work (in its contents) consisted in being friendly, happy, caring, warm, smiling, courteous and, in addition, having high standards of appearance and hygiene. Third, the significance of people/social work was its systematic connection to the production of 'successful' establishments: 'success' involving the production of ever-increasing custom.

What is very striking about this construction of work in the two workplaces is the resonances it has with both Offe's (1985) analysis of service labour and Urry's (1990) analysis of the structuring of employment relations within tourism (both discussed in Chapter 1). In particular, the emphasis at Fun Land and Global Hotel on the quality of the social interaction between the producer (employees) and the consumer (customers), the prioritizing of the work of employees in these interactions above all other aspects of their work, and the emphasis on the appropriate appearance and behaviour of employees in the delivery of this work, all seem to confirm both Offe's and Urry's analyses of the social character of service labour and, in particular, Urry's contention that the quality of the social interaction between producers and consumers is part of what is sold within the tourist industry. Thus the construction of work relations at the two workplaces suggested, as Urry has argued, that consumers' cultural expectations of service delivery may play an important part in the structuring of employment relations within tourism.

The issue of the interaction between employees and customers at Fun Land and Global Hotel will be returned to later in this chapter. First, however, it is necessary to pursue further the significance of the construction of work outlined so far, since many of the workplace practices, including recruitment and regulation and a differentiation of men and women as 'workers', were related to this account of 'work'.

Staff recruitment at Fun Land

The majority of Fun Land's employees (93 per cent) were recruited on-site during the season by various departmental managers. Over half of these seasonal workers were, however, clustered in just two departments – the parks department and the catering department, where they were employed as ride operators and catering assistants, respectively. The ride operators, or operatives, were employed to load people on and off, check safety harnesses and run the various amusement devices in the leisure park. These machines or 'fun rides' included roller coasters and circular, children's and water rides. Operatives constituted the largest single occupational category of seasonal employment, and this group was highly gender-segregated. Of 74 operatives, 66 (90 per cent) were men (see Table 1.2). The men ranged in age from 18 to 52 years; however, the average was 28 years with 59 per cent aged between 18 and 28 years (see Fig. 4.1). The women operatives also had a fairly wide age range (20–40 years), with the average being 25 years. However, even more women were clustered between the ages of 18 and 28 (75 per cent) (see Fig. 4.2). Thus both men and women operatives were relatively young.

The operators who worked the children's rides, and those who operated the other 'fun rides' (which were known throughout the park as the 'fast rides'), were segregated by gender and age. All the women employed as operatives worked on the children's rides, as did the older men (those over 36). Only the younger men, aged between 18 and 36, worked the fast rides (approximately 80 per cent of all men operatives).

The recruitment of operative staff at Fun Land was the responsibility of the parks manager, and he took on the majority of them at the beginning of the season. He used very definite criteria to assess the suitability of potential new operatives, criteria which derived from a particular construction of the operative occupation. He made a clear distinction between the fast rides (the majority) and the children's rides, and maintained they had different kinds of 'requirements' for their operation.

The requirement constructed for the operation of fast rides can be best described as 'essential maleness'. This was achieved in two ways. First, the parks manager ascribed the fast rides an 'essential' status, whereby their operation was seen to require workers to possess the vital attribute of physical strength. He argued that fast ride operatives 'need to be strong to be able to operate the [fast] rides'. Physical strength was, however, constructed as completely synonymous with maleness – only men were seen to be physically strong. The parks manager said he could not employ women on the fast rides because 'they wouldn't be able to cope with it – you need be strong to work those rides'. In addition, physical strength was not only conflated with maleness, it was also an attribute of young men. The criteria that the parks manager used for the selection of operatives for the fast rides thus derived directly from these constructions: they should be young men, 'ideally they should be like Hercules'.

On the other hand, the children's rides at Fun Land were viewed

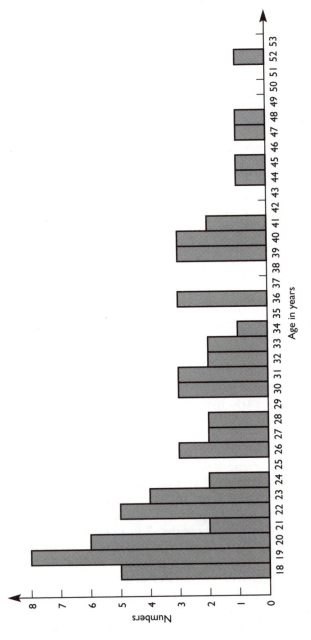

Figure 4.1 Age distribution by gender of the men operatives (seasonal): Fun Land, summer 1989 (*n*=66)

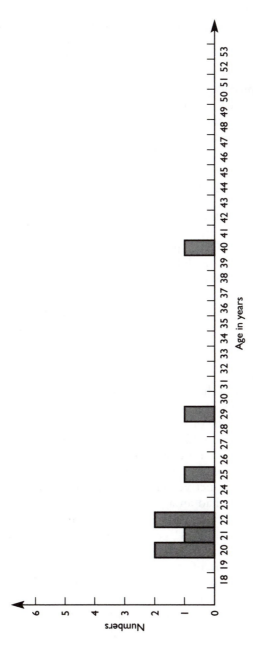

Figure 4.2 Age distribution by gender of women operatives (seasonal): Fun Land, summer 1989 (*n*=8)

not to require any particular capacities for their operation. More importantly, their operation was constructed by the parks manager in relation to the fast rides. They were constructed as not requiring physical strength, and consequently the workers who were seen to be suitable operators were those who supposedly do not possess physical strength, namely women and older men.

These constructions of the sorts of workers required for the different kinds of rides were, of course, totally dependent upon the distinction made between them and their supposedly different operational requirements. This 'distinction', however, had little material base. The actual procedures for all the rides in the park were exactly the same. They all shared an automated system of operation whereby they were activated by operatives depressing a switch. None of the operatives were required to participate in activities which required physical strength. The rides were fixed on site, so no-one was required to set up or dismantle them, unlike travelling fairs; nor did operatives have to do repairs, since maintenance staff were employed for this purpose. Nevertheless, this construction of the 'differences' between rides formed the criteria used by the parks manager to assess the 'suitability' of candidates for operative employment, and he applied them systematically.

Within the catering department, catering assistants were employed both to prepare and to serve customers food and drink in the restaurant and the various catering kiosks situated around the park. This occupation was second only in importance to that of operatives as a site of employment for seasonal staff. Catering assistants were also highly segregated by gender: out of a total of 51 assistants, 33 (65 per cent) were women and only 18 (35 per cent) were men (see Table 1.2). Like the job of operative, that of catering assistant had a distinctive gendered age distribution. Though the women assistants had an age range of 16–47 years, most (82 per cent) were aged 16–21 (see Fig. 4.3). Similarly, the men assistants had an age range of 16–41 years, but 61 per cent were aged 16–18 (see Fig. 4.4) – on average 10 years younger than the operatives.

The recruitment of catering assistants at Fun Land was the responsibility of the catering manager, and again the majority were appointed at the beginning of the season. As with the parks manager, the catering manager used a very particular set of criteria to assess the suitability of potential new catering assistants. But here

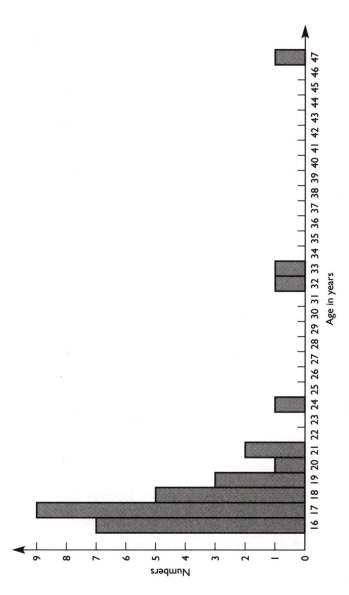

Figure 4.3 Age distribution by gender of women catering assistants (seasonal): Fun Land, summer 1989

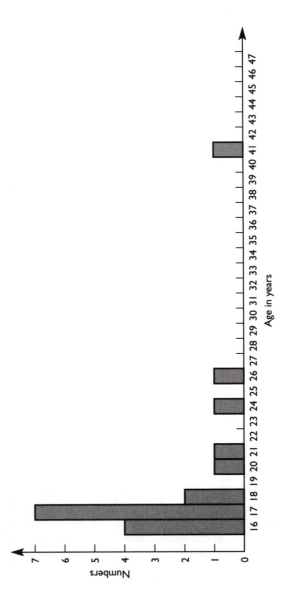

Figure 4.4 Age distribution by gender of men catering assistants (seasonal); Fun Land, summer 1989

the criteria used derived from a particular construction of *workers themselves*, rather than a set of occupational 'requirements'.

The criteria used to judge the suitability of applicants was based, quite simply, on the assumption that catering assistants would be women. Just as the position of fast ride operative was constructed as inherently male, the position of catering assistant was constructed as somehow inherently female. But while the inherent maleness of the fast ride occupation and the criteria used to recruit fast ride operatives were both achieved by producing a link between the supposed occupational requirements and men (fast rides 'need' physical strength, and young men possess such strength), no such link was provided for the catering assistant occupation. It was constructed as 'women's work' not through any link between the specificity of the occupation and women (i.e. not by any particular construction of its occupational requirements as being 'female'), but rather by the criteria used for recruitment being related to a particular construction of what women needed to be workers at Fun Land.

This construction of women workers centred on appearance. Women workers needed the 'right' appearance to be employed, and what the catering manager said she was looking for was 'brightness in their [women's] appearance' when recruiting. This 'brightness' included being 'attractive and looking fresh'. The boundaries of 'right' appearance were very tightly defined, for the catering manager had a very definite set of criteria for what constituted the 'wrong' appearance. One woman, for example, was not recruited on the grounds that she looked 'weird', this 'weirdness' being constituted by the woman wearing a scarf tied around her head 'with part of it hanging down over her face'. That fact that part of this woman's face was covered was a 'problem' as far as the catering manager was concerned, and it formed the basis for not offering her employment. The 'right' appearance therefore partly involves facial display and appropriate clothing.

Further details of what exactly constituted the 'right' appearance for women catering assistants were shown by the way in which certain women came to be employed as operatives at Fun Land. These women were constructed as having an inappropriate appearance to be employed in the occupations in which the majority of women were clustered. In particular, they 'looked wrong' to be employed as catering assistants. For example, at the beginning of the season, two young women were offered employment as operatives rather than as catering assistants because it was said, 'they were too butch, too manly'. Other women were also offered operative employment rather than work in the occupations where women were clustered because they were 'too ugly'. The two 'butch' women were aware of the way in which this set of appearance criteria was used in relation to them: 'we went in there, and she just looked us up and down and sent us to the parks manager. We knew exactly what was going on, because we knew it was happening to all the other women as well . . . and, well, it was so obvious'.

Thus women workers who were seen not to look 'right' were effectively excluded, on this basis, from being catering assistants. But although women workers were constructed as 'needing' this 'right' appearance for the position of catering assistant, this was not linked in any way to the occupation itself by the catering manager. Rather, it was linked to the general 'nature' of Fun Land's operations. According to the catering manager, it was necessary for women workers to possess these qualities 'because of the customers'. When asked why this was the case, she said simply, 'In this kind of work, it's one of the things that customers expect'.

Interaction with customers, however, was hardly specific to the position of catering assistant. Virtually all the seasonal worker occupations (barring the chefs and cooks, launderers, and sound and lighting operators, who together constituted only 2 per cent of the total seasonal staff) were characterized by 'high' customer contact. Moreover, the fact that some women who were said to have the 'wrong' appearance were offered operative employment further problematizes the claim, since the position of operative was also characterized by a high degree of customer contact. So, if women catering assistants need the right appearance 'because of the customers', how can we explain why such criteria were not being used universally?

In addition, potential men catering assistants were not subject to these kinds of appearance criteria. However, all the men who worked as catering assistants were viewed by the catering manager as 'special' or 'exceptional' and in need of explanation. This was a function of her assumption that under 'normal' circumstances women would fill all the places. The catering manager explained, for example, that by far the majority of the men who worked as catering assistants did so because they were too young to work as operatives. It is illegal for people under the age of 18 to operate fairground and amusement park rides, and as was seen above, 11 of the 18 men employed as catering assistants were under 18. These men all applied in the first instance to be operatives at Fun Land, but because of their age, the parks manager was unable to employ them in this capacity. So he directed them into other occupations, in particular into the occupations of catering and shop assistants. The majority of the men employed as catering assistants were therefore there simply because they were too young to work as operatives. These young men were treated completely differently by the catering manager from the women who applied to become catering assistants. All of the men who were passed on to her because they were too young to work as operatives were offered employment. And they were not subject to the appearance criteria applied to the women.

But then men over 18 working as catering assistants were *also* not subject to any particular employment criteria; and they were also constructed by the catering manager as 'exceptional'. They were men who 'usually wouldn't work as catering assistants but...'. These 'buts' included: two men who were doing hotel and catering courses who wanted some vocational experience; a man with health problems; and a man who wanted to work 'with' his partner, a woman who was also employed as a catering assistant.

Men catering assistants were thus regarded as unusual, and, un-like the women, their presence was seen as due either to excep-tional circumstances or to circumstances beyond their control. Most importantly, however, all these men were exempt from the appearance criteria used by the catering manager in relation to women workers, and they were always offered employment either on the basis of their 'exceptional' circumstances or because of their lack of 'choice'.

What was clear was that women workers were subject to a set of criteria relating to appearance regardless of occupation, while men were not. These criteria can be said to exist regardless of occu-pation in two senses. First, they existed not because the occupation 'needed' its workers to possess these qualities – you do not have to be pretty to make sandwiches – but because women workers were constructed as somehow needing these appearance qualities *to be workers*. Despite the catering manager's insistence that women workers were subject to these criteria 'because of the customers', this explanation is difficult to sustain. It does not explain why it was that only catering assistants needed these qualities (since customers were not specific to the catering assistant occupation), nor why it was only women who were subject to these criteria. (If these qualities were needed, then presumably the same kinds of appearance criteria should have also been applied to the men.)

The manner in which women became operatives reveals the second way in which these criteria can be said to exist regardless of occupation, since women also became operatives precisely because of the existence of appearance criteria. In other words, these criteria (as far as the catering assistants and the women operatives were concerned), to some extent at least, determined the gendered constitution of the occupations themselves. Moreover, in other departments at Fun Land, the appearance of women workers also formed the single most important criterion for employment. As one women operative said, 'women working in the bar were just chosen for what they look like. He [the bars manager] would just employ women who he liked the look of, who he fancied. All the women working in the bar knew it as well'.

Staff recruitment at Global Hotel

Recruitment of all staff below the level of departmental manager at Global Hotel was also an on-site activity. But unlike Fun Land, the personnel manager was solely responsible for all recruitment. The recruitment process itself was governed by a set of company-produced criteria for workers within each occupation. These criteria were known within the hotel as 'personnel specifications' and they were produced at the UK headquarters. The personnel manager was bound by company policy to adhere to them during recruitment.

The personnel specifications laid down what were termed the 'necessary characteristics' of workers for the different occupations in all of the company's hotels, including such characteristics as aspects of appearance, attitude and speech. According to Global Hotel's operations manual (which outlined all hotel procedures), the purpose of these specifications was to 'enable the recruiter to have an objective picture of the person needed to fill the vacancy'.

Attention to these personnel specifications reveals that the construction of men and women as workers at Global Hotel took a very similar form to Fun Land.

Table 4.1 shows the personnel specifications in operation in relation to seven of the nine occupations for which the personnel manager at Global Hotel had recruitment responsibility. These seven occupations were all highly gender-segregated at Global Hotel. The kitchen hands and porters were exclusively men, whereas the receptionists and housekeepers were all women. The chefs, cooks, bar staff and waiting staff, although not exclusively segregated by gender, showed high degrees of segregation, with men constituting 87 per cent of chefs and cooks and 73 per cent of bar staff, and women 71 per cent of waiting staff (see Table 1.4).

What is most striking about the personnel specifications in relation to gender segregation is that those relating to occupations in which women were clustered (waitress, receptionist and housekeeper) show remarkable continuity. According to the specifications, all these occupations 'require' workers to be 'attractive', of

Table 4.1 Personnel specifications of selected occupations: Global Hotel

Occupation	Specifications
Chef/cook	Clear speech
	Good social skills: must be a good communicator with both guests and staff
Kitchen hand	Average height and weight
	Clean, well turned out
Waitress	Attractive
	Average height and weight
	Must have helpful enthusiastic attitude
Receptionist	Attractive
	Average weight and height
	Must have helpful enthusiastic attitude
Barman	Strong
	Average weight and height
	Very smart, able to communicate well with general public, enthusiastic and helpful manner
Domestic	Attractive
	Average weight and height
	Must have helpful enthusiastic attitude
Porter	Strong
	Average height and weight

'average height and weight', and to have a 'helpful and enthusiastic attitude'. Indeed, all of these occupations have the same personnel specifications. They are interchangeable.

In contrast, the specifications for the occupations in which men were clustered (chef/cook, kitchen hand, barman and porter) show no real continuity. Unlike the occupations in which women workers were clustered, the specifications for occupations in which men were clustered are varied, with no two occupations sharing the same set of specifications. Some of the occupations have some specifications in common, but the majority (three out of four) have their own specific requirements.

What is also notable is that the occupations at Global Hotel in which women were clustered, have one specific specification not found in relation to any occupation in which men are clustered: namely being 'attractive'. Some of the requirements common to 'women's occupations' are also found in some 'men's occupations' (i.e. the requirement to be of an average height, or to be helpful and enthusiastic). But being 'attractive' never operates in relation to *any* of the 'men's' occupations. It therefore stands out as a requirement specific to women.

In comparing the personnel specifications with the gendered organization of occupations, it is not being suggested that the specifications in and of themselves explain the forms of gendered occupational segregation which existed. Indeed, since the specifications themselves clearly assume an already gender-segregated occupational structure – they assume, for example, that bar staff will be men ('barmen') and that waiting staff will be women ('waitresses') – any such claim is clearly precluded. But the fact that the specifications do make these assumptions provides valuable insights into the construction of men and women as workers at Global Hotel. The fact, for example, that all the occupations in which women are clustered have the same specifications, and in particular that the specification about being attractive only operates in relation to 'women's occupations', suggests these specifications are requirements which operate in relation to women workers *generally*, regardless of occupation, rather than in relation to any particular occupational requirements.

This claim, that it is women as workers who are subject to this requirement, is strengthened if the task content, the specifications and the gender constitution of two comparable occupations – bar staff and waiting staff – are considered. Both these occupations were highly gender-segregated, with men constituting by far the majority of bar staff and women by far the majority of waiting staff. The task content of these occupations was, however, remarkably similar. They were both 'high customer contact' occupations: they both involved taking orders from customers and serving them with either drinks (bar staff), or food and/or drinks (waiting staff). Given these similarities, it might seem likely that the personnel specifications would require similar sorts of worker qualities. In certain respects, this was the case, in that in both occupations workers were required to be helpful and enthusiastic, and of average height and weight. Bar staff, however, unlike waiting staff, are required to be strong, to be smart and to have good communication skills, whereas waiting staff, unlike bar staff, are required to be attractive.

This difference in occupational specifications cannot be adequately explained by 'different' requirements of the occupations themselves. Why, for example, should strength be a requirement of bar staff and not of waiting staff when delivering food and drink to tables all day requires physical strength and stamina and is as physically demanding and exhausting as lifting crates and changing barrels in bar work? Why were bar staff only required to be smart (that is, to have smart clothes), whereas waiting staff needed to have a visually attractive personal appearance? (In any case, workers in both of these occupations have to wear 'smart' uniforms.) These occupations were so similar that the differences in their personnel specifications made little sense in terms of the occupations themselves.

This lends further weight to the proposition that all the occupations in which women were clustered shared the same requirement to be 'attractive' precisely *because* these occupations were filled either exclusively or primarily by women. In other words, the specifications related to the gender of the occupants of the occupations, rather than to the requirements of the occupations themselves. It was women as workers who were subject to this requirement across all occupations, rather than particular occupations requiring this quality. The fact that the specifications for all the occupations in which men were clustered systematically did not include a requirement to be attractive, even when tasks within an occupation were strikingly similar to occupations in which women were clustered, further suggests that it is women as workers who are constructed as 'needing' this quality, regardless of occupation.

Men, however, were not only exempt from the requirement to be attractive, they were also not constructed as needing any other particular qualities as a group. The specifications relating to the occupations in which men were clustered were diverse, and although some occupations shared some specifications, the majority had their own particular occupational requirements. The requirements to which men were subject operated at the level of specific occupations.

When asked why this particular requirement operated only in relation to all women employees, the personnel manager at Global Hotel replied in a similar vein to the catering manager at Fun Land: it was 'the sort of thing needed in the hotel trade because impressions employees make on customers and the kinds of services provided can make a big difference [for custom]'. But again this argument simply did not explain why it was that only women were subject to this requirement if they wished to be workers at Global Hotel.

These common findings from Fun Land and Global Hotel, especially the ways in which women workers were constructed as a distinct and unified group of workers, are consistent with other studies which have also been concerned with the conditions of women's service employment. In her study of secretaries, for example, Pringle (1989a, 1989b) found that the construction of women workers as secretaries does not relate to the tasks involved in being a secretary (such as typing, word processing or filing), but rather relates to what secretaries are as women. Thus as mentioned in Chapter 2, she found three main such constructions: office wives, mothers and daughters. Similarly, in their research on women's part-time work across both service and manufacturing occupations, Beechey and Perkins (1987) found that regardless of their jobs, women part-time workers are always defined as marginal workers.

In a similar vein, a number of recent studies point to ways in which women's employment is connected to sets of criteria relating to women *as women*. Rees (1992), for instance, has discussed the ways in which those responsible for recruitment are reassured when women applying for professional positions have a feminine appearance. Rees argues this is especially the case for occupations usually dominated by men, and for grades of jobs which women rarely reach. More dramatically, in her pioneering study of flight attendants in the USA, Hochschild (1983) exposed the ways in which women were subject to a specific set of recruitment criteria relating to their appearance from which men were exempt. Thus, potential women stewardesses had to conform to certain specified standards for 'weight, figure, straight teeth, complexion, facial regularity, [and] age' (Hochschild 1983: 96) before they were even allowed to proceed to job interviews. Indeed, in numerous studies of recruitment procedures for airline attendants, physical attractiveness has been found to be the most important criteria for women's employment. Thus, Singapore's national airline, for example, only recruits women who are 'slim and attractive with a clear complexion, taller than 1.58 metres, with a smile' (Bellos 1991: 24); and various Australian airlines use 'physical beauty' and 'appeal' as key recruitment criteria (Williams 1988: 95-6). Moreover, the same appearance criteria have been shown *not* to operate for potential men stewards. Thus Williams found potential men stewards to be rarely subject to criteria regarding their appearance, while women are systematically screened and have to reach a whole range of appearance standards, including standards relating to weight, height, and complexion (Williams 1988: 93-6). To become workers, women flight attendants as a group are thus subject to a set of criteria relating to appearance from which men are exempt.

Moreover, as at Fun Land and Global Hotel, the conditions attached to women's employment seem to have little or no connection with the actual tasks involved in being an airline attendant. We might ask, for instance, why women are required to be attractive to serve meals to passengers or to sell them duty free goods in flight? But like the managers at Global Hotel and Fun Land, various managers in the airline industry stress that these qualities are required because of the attendants' role in customer relations. Airline attendants are viewed as a vital 'part of the packaging of the product' (Williams 1988: 96).

Men and women workers and 'people' work

At Fun Land and Global Hotel, we saw that there were a number of important continuities between customer relations or the 'people' work deemed so important for their success, and the different constructions of men and women workers at the two worksites. For instance, high personal standards, especially in relation to appearance and hygiene, were viewed as necessary for successful 'people' work, and one aspect – the appearance of workers – was shown to be integral to the construction of workers at both workplaces. In addition, this significance was highly gender-specific. Women as a group, at both Global Hotel and Fun Land, were systematically subject to specific requirements in relation to appearance. Men, on the other hand, were either excluded from these (and any parallel requirements) or, as at Global Hotel, some men were subject to specific appearance requirements in relation to particular occupations.

Certain elements within the construction of 'work' (those relating to appearance) thus operated only in relation to women workers, but they were central to the way in which women workers were constructed. These continuities between the construction of 'work' and the construction of 'women workers' suggest that women play a very particular role in the 'people' work ascribed such significance at both worksites. Women workers had to be attractive at Global Hotel, and 'look good' at Fun Land. In other words, these continuities suggest that the construction of 'women workers' at Global Hotel and Fun Land relate to women being ascribed a particular role within the arena of customer relations.

This raises a number of related issues. The significance of customer relations (or 'people' work) is closely connected with the production of profit at both worksites. Such work (supposedly) encourages custom. The most obvious conclusion to be drawn from this would be that, at both worksites, women as workers are constructed as a group whose members need to look attractive, and are subject to criteria relating to this requirement because this 'quality' encourages custom, and therefore increased sales. These constructions and related criteria are, in other words, functional for capital.

This does not explain, however, why it is that only women are subject to such criteria. Presumably, if these 'qualities' can increase custom, then men as workers should be subject to the same kinds of criteria to maximize the potential for the accumulation of profit. If only women are seen to 'need' these qualities, then it becomes problematic how customer relations/'people' work is linked to the production of profit.

The regulation of workers

The appearance of women workers at Fun Land and Global Hotel was not simply at issue during recruitment. It was also subject to some considerable attention once women were in employment. At both workplaces, workers were subject to regulations and controls on their appearance. At Fun Land, for instance, one of the main regulations was the compulsory wearing of uniforms. Failure to wear a uniform, or the incorrect wearing of a uniform, by seasonal workers while at work was a dismissable offence. The exact form of the uniform was decided by the departmental managers. At Fun Land, both men and women operatives wore a military style uniform consisting of trousers and a tunic with gold braids and buttons, while women catering assistants wore black knee-length skirts, white blouses and catering aprons, and men catering assistants black trousers, white shirts and full-length catering aprons. Other uniforms at Fun Land included checked gingham dresses, worn by women bar staff and by women working as dancers in the parks department, and black trousers and white shirts, worn by glass collectors and men bar staff.

In addition to the compulsory wearing of uniforms, staff were also asked to conform to numerous other standards of appearance and behaviour. These were presented to employees in an employee handbook. The following excerpts are typical:

> Your Hair: Keep it clean, so that customers find it a pleasure to look at. Keep it off your face so that customers can see you when talking to you.

> Your Personal Freshness: Three danger points are Breath, Underarms, Feet. And what about the other parts we never talk about.

> Your Hands and Fingernails: It goes without saying that

hands and nails are clean, but how well manicured are your nails? Do you bite them? Do you have nicotine stains? In what state is your nail varnish?

Some points in you appearance and your work area which the customer will notice are: The state of your collar and cuffs. Whether your uniform fits. If your buttons are all fastened. Your fingernails. Untidy hairstyles, beards or moustache. Laddered tights. Clean Shoes. Neatly pressed clothes.

Your posture can indicate very clearly to a customer whether or not you are going to be helpful . . . The way we sit, the way we stand, the posture we adopt, leaning on elbows, not standing straight on two feet, folding arms, the gestures we make, fidgeting with jewellery, tapping fingers, looking at watches, yawning, picking nose, biting nails or scratching, all give the customer an impression of boredom or couldn't care less.

Use your eyes! It is polite to look at the person who is talking to you (but avoid staring – it's rude) . . . Use your ears! Listen carefully to what your customer is saying to you.

Use your mouth! A smile, especially when greeting a customer, can be the greatest customer relations exercise of all.

Your first words create an impression which colour the customer's reply . . . Remember to be heard and understood you need to speak clearly and look at the customer as you speak.

Please remember our customers come here to enjoy them-selves. You can spoil the visit by being rude and careless, or you can help them have a good time by being friendly and helpful . . . the standard of service you give will determine whether or not our customers come back time and time again or leave never to return again.

What is noticeable about these standards, is the way conforming to them is presented as part of the job of seasonal workers. But in constructing these standards as worker responsibilities ('You can spoil the visit by . . .'), what management is equally saying is that any failure to meet the standards means workers are not doing their jobs properly, and is a matter for employer intervention. As such, naming and labelling areas of employee appearance and behaviour as somehow significant, and the responsibility of the workers, provides a surface upon which regulation, administration and intervention in these areas can occur.

This was confirmed in the day-to-day practices of departmental managers at Fun Land. The parks manager, for example, spent most of his time walking the park, 'checking up on them [the seasonal workers]'. He said the primary aim of this 'checking up' was to ensure that workers were behaving themselves. He made sure they kept to the 'rules', which, he argued, he was 'hard and fast' about. Contravention of these 'rules' by seasonal workers constituted punishable offences, with the parks manager 'handing out punishments to fit the crime'.

Seasonal workers at Fun Land confirmed his high level of regulative practice in relation to both their behaviour and appearance. One woman operative, for example, described how the parks manager 'was always walking around the park checking on us [the women operatives] and constantly giving us warnings about things like the state of our uniforms, if we didn't have all the buttons done up or if they were dirty' and 'he often used the threat of sacking us for those kinds of things'. The parks manager also constantly gave warnings to the young men operatives not to 'chat up' women customers. He found this aspect of the operatives' behaviour a particular problem, and one which was difficult to control.

During the season when my fieldwork took place, the parks manager did dismiss a number of operatives on the grounds of behaviour and appearance offences. These included the dismissal of one man operative for 'chatting up' women customers, another man operative for arguing with customers and with the parks manager himself, a third man operative for being drunk on duty, a woman operative for being, as he said, 'too domineering', and another woman operative for the incorrect wearing of her uniform.

Similarly, within the catering department, the catering manager was also concerned to ensure that seasonal workers conformed to 'correct' codes of appearance and behaviour, and, as with the parks manager, a considerable amount of her supervisory time was dedicated to these issues. She saw workers conforming to these 'correct codes' as of vital importance for the successful functioning of the catering department, and she regarded it as part of her job in managing the department to ensure that they did.

The methods used by the catering manager to ensure conformity also included the use of formal warnings, the threat of dismissal, and dismissal itself. During the fieldwork, for example, she consistently used verbal warnings, in particular in relation to workers being 'sloppy in their appearance' and for behavioural 'offences'. More specifically, she often warned women workers about aspects of their appearance: about not 'looking right' . One woman, for example, was warned because of 'the state of her nail varnish', while another was warned because her general appearance 'just went downhill... She was OK at first, but just got worse. But once she was told, she got better. She just had to be reminded to take more care'. Two men catering assistants were also warned consistently about 'always being really dirty' while on duty. She also regularly warned another man catering assistant for arguing with the customers.

The catering manager dismissed a number of workers on the grounds of appearance and behaviour problems, including one woman worker for consistently wearing 'weird' make-up: '... tons of white powder all over her face, and loads of dark red lipstick ... and sometimes she had thick black eyeliner coming right out over her face ... She looked really horrible, like a ghost'. When this woman started to wear this make-up the catering manager warned her not to wear it again at work, but she continued to do so. In the end, the catering manager argued she had 'no choice' but to dismiss her because 'you can't look like that here'. Another woman catering assistant was also dismissed on the grounds of appearance problems. The catering manager said that as soon as this woman got the job she just seemed to 'let herself [her appearance] go' . This 'letting herself go' included consistently looking 'sloppy' and tired, 'as if she had just got out of bed ... At times she looked a real mess'. This woman too was given warnings about 'her' 'problems' by the manager, but did not respond. 'The only thing to do after all this', the catering manager said, 'was to sack her'.

What was notable in the overall regulation of workers'

appearance and behaviour was that men and women were subject to different forms of regulation. Men were far more likely to be subject to intervention in relation to their behaviour than women, and women far more likely to be subject to intervention in relation to their appearance. In addition, the forms of appearance problems which women catering assistants had which were subject to regulation were qualitatively different from those of their men colleagues. The two men catering asssistants were both said to be 'dirty'. This dirtiness constituted a threat to hygiene within the department, and it became a matter of concern when customers began to complain about it. That is to say, these were problems based upon a concern with hygiene rather than a concern with visual appearance. In contrast, instances in which women catering assistants were regulated were all based specifically on the grounds of visual appearance in and of itself. Moreover, each was based upon contravention of a particular set of criteria operating in relation to women's appearance – criteria which did not operate in relation to men.

The existence of these criteria is revealed by the rationale used to justify such intervention in the appearance of women workers. In all the cases where the catering manager intervened, she explained the regulation in terms of women workers 'not looking right'. She located all the cases as being forms of appearance that were a problem because 'you can't look like that here': you can't wear 'weird' make-up, chipped nail varnish, look tired, and so on.

This is further demonstrated by a consideration of who was warned and who was dismissed and for what. The catering manager dismissed women workers because of their appearance, but none of the men she regulated was dismissed – only warned. That is, not only were men exempt from appearance regulation, but even when they had other 'problems' they were still not subject to the same degrees of regulation as women. This was not because what they did was less of a problem than what women did: on the contrary, their behaviour was unquestionably more problematic. For instance, in the case of the men catering assistants being 'dirty', their 'dirtiness' was a recurrent problem, and the catering manager consistently warned them about it because it was contravening hygiene laws. Similarly, the man who was warned for arguing with customers was warned repeatedly for something that was contrary to company policy.

While men only got warned for continuing or repeated problems, such 'problems' with women workers were likely to result in dismissal. Men who did not respond to warnings continued to have problems. They were consistently warned – but not dismissed. Even in cases where men consistently posed various problems they were never subject to dismissal. In this sense, men catering assistants appeared to be almost 'unconditional' workers in relation to appearance and behaviour. Their status as workers was never threatened.

On the other hand, the women catering assistants were subject to a set of criteria relating to their appearance from which men were exempt, *and* contravention of the criteria led to forms of management intervention, including dismissal. Adherence to these appearance criteria was therefore a condition of work for such women. To retain their position, they were compelled to maintain the 'right' appearance.

Men operatives were also exempt from appearance regulations. All of the forms of intervention to which men were subject related to their behaviour, and in particular to problematic forms of interaction with customers, including chatting them up and arguing with them. But unlike men catering assistants, men operatives were subject to dismissal for these behavioural problems. Women operatives were also subject to forms of intervention relating to behaviour (in particular, one woman was dismissed for being 'too domineering'), but it was the appearance of women operatives which was more often the subject of regulation, especially uniform 'problems'.

Although there was this continuity across the two occupations, there were also important differences between them in terms of the forms of behaviour and appearance which were subject to gendered regulation. The regulation of women operatives' appearance was, for example, different from that of catering assistants. Women catering assistants had to conform to prescribed standards which meant their appearance was under a specific form of regulative control. For women operatives, however, such regulation focused only upon their uniforms. They were allowed to wear 'weird' make-up, to look as if they had just got up, or 'let their appearance go', so long as their uniforms were worn correctly. The maintenance of the right 'attractive' appearance was not a condition of employment for them.

The regulation of men and women as 'workers'

What stands out from these different forms of regulation is that there are a number of continuities between them and the constructions of men and women as workers discussed earlier in relation to the occupations of catering assistant and operative. For example, it was shown that the few women who were employed as operatives were not qualified to be employed in the occupations in which most of the women at Fun Land were clustered. They had the 'wrong' appearance to work in 'women's jobs'. There is thus a direct relationship between the initial construction of women operatives as having the 'wrong' appearance, and the forms of regulation to which they were then subject. The manner in which these women come to be operatives (that is, by possessing the 'wrong' appearance) determined the forms of regulative control in relation to appearance to which they were subsequently subject.

With men catering assistants, a similar relationship existed. As was established earlier, these men were constructed as 'special' cases, who under 'normal' circumstances would not fill such posts. This 'special' status also determined the forms of regulation to which they were subject, for they retained their position even when they posed particular problems. Their initial 'special' status was thus maintained within the workplace itself.

For women operatives, and men catering assistants, there was thus a direct relationship between their construction as workers and the forms of regulative control to which their group of workers was subject. This relationship is perhaps most clear in the case of women catering assistants. As has been demonstrated, being a catering assistant is constructed as somehow inherently female: it is a 'woman's occupation'. The recruitment of (mostly) women workers to its ranks comes not from a link between what the occupation requires and what women can do; rather, the recruitment of women workers is organized by criteria relating to appearance. The forms of appearance regulation to which women catering assistants were subject once they were employed were clearly based on the same criteria as structured their recruitment in the first place. Recruitment was based upon women 'looking good', and the forms of regulation to which women catering assistants were subject derived from this construction of the 'right' appearance. The 'right' appearance which structured recruitment consisted in women looking visually attractive and fresh, and regulations operating inside the workplace aimed to maintain this.

This, and other examples quoted earlier, demonstrate that women's continued employment was conditional upon their maintaining the visually attractive appearance used as the criterion for their recruitment. Since women not only had to look good to be employed, but also had to keep looking good as a condition of remaining employed, and since across occupations they had no choice but to adhere to certain standards of appearance, it can be said that *part of the job* for women consisted in looking good.

This was also the case at Global Hotel. Once employed, women in all occupations were obliged to conform to a plethora of standards relating to their personal appearance in ways which men were not. Women employees were given strict guidelines on the way they should look, including how they should wear their hair (to ensure facial display), how to wear make-up, and in what manner to wear their uniforms (which included sheer stockings and shoes with heels). Failure to adhere to these standards again led to forms of management intervention, including warnings and the possibility of dismissal. Women workers were, in other words, specifically subject to a set of controls and conditions relating to their personal visual appearance which sought to produce an 'attractive' female workforce.

Global Hotel specifies its requirements for the appearance of employees in a series of manuals. Women, for example, are instructed to:

> Arrive promptly for duty at 7.00 am dressed in uniform: navy blue skirt, white/blue blouse, blue or black shoes. Hair should be clean and tied away from face if long. Tights in a neutral colour, stockings and shoes should be well cared for. A minimum of jewellery to be worn. Entire appearance is to look attractive, clean and fresh.

While men are asked to:

> Arrive promptly for duty at 7 am wearing Global Limited uniform: navy blue trousers, white shirt, navy blue jacket. Shoes and socks should be black or navy blue.

The difference between the requirements of men and women in relation to appearance at Global Hotel is clear. The standards operating for men exclude precisely those which are concerned with personal appearance. Both men and women must wear clean uniforms, but this was *all* men were required to do. Men were not required to look 'attractive, clean and fresh', nor did they have to ensure they displayed their faces (by pulling their hair away from their face). The *personal* appearance of the men was simply not a subject of concern: their looks were not the subject of attention and being attractive was neither their entry qualification nor a condition of their continued employment. For the women at Global Hotel, as at Fun Land, part of their job involved maintaining an attractive appearance. They had to 'exchange' this – that is, to meet the conditions of 'attractiveness' – in return for employment.

This compulsion on women to maintain an 'attractive' appearance is also evident in other service jobs. To be employed as an airline attendant, women must fulfil a range of criteria relating to their appearance, and they must maintain their 'appeal' and 'beauty' as a condition of their employment. Up until 1985, for instance, women flight attendants were weighed to ensure they did not exceed the desired weight and could be fired for being one pound 'over weight' (Hochschild 1983: 102; Williams 1988: 92). This practice has now ended (after much struggle), but women still have their appearance tightly controlled and regulated. They are asked, for instance, to take 'cosmetic leave' if they have a problem with their appearance and can only resume employment when the 'problem' is resolved. In her study in Australia, for example, Williams (1988) found that women were asked to take leave when their complexion deviated from the prescribed standards (for instance, by having spots). In addition, women flight attendants have also been dismissed for having the 'wrong' hairstyle (for example, curly instead of straight hair) and for failing to wear make-up (Williams 1988; Maitland 1991). Needless to say, men stewards have not been found to have such conditions attached to their employment (Williams 1988).

Appearance criteria also operate for other women working in the airline industry. Women ticket agents are subject to a whole series of controls regarding their appearance, and like the women 'in the air' they must maintain an 'appealing' appearance as a condition of their employment. For instance, they must wear make-up on the job, and failure to do so can lead to dismissal. In 1991, for example, a ticket agent for Continental Airlines in the USA was sacked for 'violating the company's professional standards regulations': not because she was a bad clerk, but because she did not wear make-up (Maitland 1991).

Indeed, such appearance criteria operate across the commercial service sector for women. Woolf (1990), for instance, lists a whole catalogue of such regulations. She documents how women newsreaders are required to be attractive as a condition of their employment, and may be sacked for being 'too old and too unattractive'; how women booksellers may be fired for wearing trousers to work; how waitresses have been fired for 'losing their image'; how women casino workers have lost their jobs for attempting to resist wearing a uniform consisting of a mini-skirt and blouse with a plunging neckline; and how women retail managers may be asked to make certain specified changes in their appearance (for example, 'from the neck up') to keep their jobs. Woolf also records the ways in which men are exempt from such appearance criteria. Men news presenters, for example, do not have their jobs threatened if they look too old, and men waiters are not fired for 'losing their image'.

The specific requirement that women have and maintain a particular bodily appearance does not, therefore, operate in particular jobs or particular workplaces; rather, it is a common requirement operating in relation to women's employment. Indeed, even where there are no formal regulations operating in relation to women's appearance, women employees often feel compelled to dress or present themselves in a particular way. In her recent study of a large retail company in Britain, Cockburn (1991) found that women office workers felt compelled to have an overall feminine appearance, and required to wear skirts or dresses with high- to medium-heeled shoes even though they were not formally asked to do so. If they wore trousers or flat-heeled shoes they were made to feel ill-at-ease and that they were inappropriately dressed.

What, then, is the significance of the requirement for women to produce and maintain an attractive visual appearance as a condition of their employment? To answer this question, I turn once again to the case of Fun Land, and in particular to the ways in which the majority of women workers are routinely sexualized by men, including customers, co-workers and managers.

The sexualization of women by men co-workers

As has been made clear, within the catering department at Fun Land the catering manager devoted a lot of time to ensuring her catering assistants maintained the 'right' appearance. The 1989 season was a 'very good one' in that the majority of the women catering assistants 'had very high [appearance] standards'. But although 1989 was a 'good' year for women workers, it was no different from previous years for the catering manager as regards the 'disgusting behaviour' of the men operatives. During their breaks, the men operatives used the restaurant facilities at Fun Land, and at such times the women catering assistants and the catering manager herself were subject to 'constant abuse'.

This abuse included the men constantly trying to chat up the women and making comments regarding aspects of their appearance, with clear sexual innuendoes. One woman catering assistant, for example, said that the operatives were 'always hassling us [the women workers], eyeing us up, trying to get us to go out with them and stuff like that . . . and they were always making comments out loud about things like our sex lives . . . whether or not they thought we'd be good in bed'. Another woman catering assistant went on, 'but if we ignored them it seemed to make them worse . . . they'd get even worse, and wouldn't stop'. Such forms of behaviour on the part of the operatives was a daily occurrence. All the women catering assistants interviewed spoke of this behaviour as unwanted, and although some said they would sometimes try to 'laugh it off', it was so routine that many of them said it was difficult to maintain this approach.

Although the forms the men operatives' behaviour took varied, it was always sexualizing behaviour. It was all a form of unwanted sexual attention, or sexual harassment. This routine sexual harassment by the men operatives of the women catering assistants caused the women workers and the catering manager great distress – not least because as the catering manager said, 'there was nothing we could do about it . . . I constantly complained to the parks manager, but he didn't do anything. He even used to laugh about it. And I complained to the general manager and he didn't do anything either . . . and [the operatives] never took any notice of me. If I tried to stop them, it would just make them worse. They'd make out it was all a laugh . . . they even did it to me'.

When they reflected on the forms and degree of harassment to which they were subjected, both the catering manager and the women catering assistants shared remarkably similar sentiments about why the operatives engaged in these practices. The catering manager said: 'They seem to think it's part of their job to do it to us, and to the customers'. Similarly, one of the women catering assistants commented: 'It's like they think it's their right, because they work on the park. That's why they hate it when we don't like it because they just think they should be able to'.

Sexual harassment by the men operatives was not confined to the women catering assistants, however. Women in various occupations experienced harassment as a routine feature of working at Fun Land. One woman member of the bar staff, for example, said that walking through the park (where the operative work stations are located) 'felt like being in a tits and bums show . . . [the operatives] would eye us up, and shout to us across the park. Things like "come and work on my ride". In addition to the park space, which was identified by women workers as a particularly dangerous site for harassment, the 'clock-in point', where all seasonal workers had to clock in and out on a daily basis, was also a location for routine sexual harassment.

The women who worked in the bars were also subject to regular sexual attention from the bars manager, who was 'always ready to try something on'. These women were particularly disturbed by the uniform requirement in their department. The bars manager insisted they wear their dresses pulled down 'off the shoulder', claiming that this was the correct way to wear them. The women were distressed by this requirement, as they felt it was degrading and that it was used by the manager to 'try to turn us into sex toys or something'. They were equally concerned about the way in which this uniform requirement was aggressively enforced by the bars manager. He would often pull their dresses down into this position. On one occasion, a woman operative reported that she entered the bar at a moment when the bars manager was trying to pull a woman's dress down over her shoulders and the woman in question 'just turned round and screamed at him "I'm not a fucking prostitute, I'm here to serve drinks" '.

However, although the women workers classified the behaviour of the men operatives and the bars manager at Fun Land as particularly aggressive, and definitely harassment, they nevertheless dealt with different sorts of sexualization on a regular basis and saw these as different in form. Men constantly referred to women's contact with other men workers in a sexualized manner. In these situations, the women often 'entered into it' and joked with the men about their various suggestions. But they did so in such a way as to move them off the subject. When one man worker (a maintenance man) was 'joking' about a woman wanting to speak to the general manager (implying that there was a sexual element), she joked with him that he was only suggesting this because he was jealous as the general manager was going to get some of her attention and he wasn't. But she then changed the subject by talking about the issue she needed to discuss with the general manager and asked his opinion about it. Another man worker (in this case a manager) 'joked' that one woman worker looked miserable because she hadn't got her 'oats' the night before. He went on to suggest that she should go out with him instead and she then wouldn't have the problem. She replied that she thought 'he wouldn't have the stamina', and told him that when she thought he did, she might reconsider his offer. This kind of sexual banter, where men workers sexualized the activities of women, was very common. The parks manager, for instance, would often say such things to women seasonal workers as, 'Where are you going? I know to see your boyfriend ... I've seen the way you look at [a particular man operative]'.

The women operatives saw and commented on the ways in which men workers routinely sexualized and harassed most of the other women workers. One said that the operatives treated most of the women who worked at Fun Land 'as if they were only there for them ... as if they were slags or something'. But they themselves were not subject to such sexualization. They were not, for instance, subject to the same routine sexual comments, leering and innuendoes as other women workers. They were, however, subject to physically threatening behaviour from the operatives which other women did not experience. They were particularly distressed, for example, by the way groups of men operatives would sometimes surround them when they were enclosed in the boxes from which they operated the children's rides. Although this practice was not routine, it nevertheless was very frightening and threatening: 'It wasn't so much that they would do anything, it was just really scary'. What concerned the women operatives most, what made this behaviour so threatening, was that they felt the men were being sexually aggressive. One woman operative, for example, said that when the men came over to her box, she felt 'there was no guarantee of not being raped'. This fear of violence was also experienced by the women operatives when they had to leave their boxes to do such things as use the toilet or go to isolated parts of the park. They were frightened that the men operatives would follow them 'and try something [violent/threatening]'.

One of the ways in which women operatives attempted to resist this threat of sexual violence was by 'sticking together': trying to go to tea breaks with at least one other woman operative, and when they had to go to isolated areas in the park trying to ensure that they went with another woman. They found, however, that the parks manager prevented them from being able to 'stick together'. For example, when two women operatives first started work at Fun Land, they made sure they had their tea breaks at the same time. But 'when [the parks manager] realized what we were doing, he wouldn't let us have our breaks together'. This action on the part of the parks manager was not in any way explicable by time management, for a system of cover operated over the break periods. It did not matter who went off with whom, at what time, as the machines never stood idle. The women felt, therefore, that the parks manager was employing strategies to prevent them from sticking together.

Such a situation – in which the women felt the parks manager was colluding in the antagonism against them – meant that on the whole they felt that 'there was no point in trying to complain'. However, one woman operative did complain to the parks manager about the behaviour of the men operatives, and did so regularly and persistently. She was the woman the parks manager dismissed, on the grounds that she was 'too domineering'.

What was interesting, however, was that although many of the women interviewed explicitly located the sexualizing or aggressive behaviour of the men operatives (and, among women in the bar, the behaviour of the bars manager) as a definite violation – as forms of behaviour they should not have to deal with when working at Fun Land – and although they found the banter of other men workers tiresome at times and to be deflected, they viewed similar behaviour from men customers in a completely different way.

The sexualization of women workers by men customers

Both the catering manager and the women catering assistants were also subject to forms of sexual attention from men customers on a daily basis. This attention again included verbal harassment, for example sexual teasing, jokes and pressure for sexual favours, and also some physical forms of sexual attention, including deliberate touching of breasts and also rubbing their bodies against the women. But the most common forms were chatting up and 'eyeing up'. The latter involves sexual objectification – treating a person as if they were an object which the observer has a right to gaze at for as long as, and in whatever way, pleases him. It frequently includes focusing upon a particular part of the body, but in a way which attempts to get the person objectified to agree to the process and to be flattered by it – to accept it as an expression of sexual interest.

One woman catering assistant reported these forms of behaviour as being directed at her by men customers on a regular basis. The men customers 'were always eyeing us up' and often 'saying things about our appearance', commenting on 'the way we looked in our uniforms . . . how they liked the way we looked in them'. Another woman catering assistant said men customers would often try to chat up the women workers: 'they were always trying to get us to meet them in the bar after work'. The women frequently found some of the things men customers said and did highly offensive. For example, when they were serving them, the men would say things like 'a plate of chips and a blow job please', or 'rubbing themselves against us when we were clearing the tables, and making out it was accidental'. The women catering assistants said these forms of sexual attention made them feel as if they were primarily defined as sex objects: 'They [the men customers] just seem to think we are on display for them, that we were there just for their benefit'.

But despite the fact that these forms of sexual attention from customers were similar to those from operatives, the catering manager made a distinction between them. She 'expected' women workers to be able to cope with sexual behaviour and attention from men customers as 'part of the job'. She said that if 'the women catering assistants complain, or say things like they can't cope, I tell them it happens all the time and not to worry about it . . . it's part of the job . . . if they can't handle it then they're not up to working here'.

Although they often found sexual attention from men customers as problematic as that from men workers, in particular the way its routine nature consistently undermined and denied their status as employees, the women catering assistants also made a distinction between the two. They too read them in completely different ways. They, like the catering manager, felt that being able to cope with these forms of attention from men customers was somehow part of the job. One woman catering assistant said of this aspect of their work: 'You just have to get used to it. It's hard sometimes, but you just have to . . . you learn to expect it'.

Women workers in other departments also echoed these sentiments. A woman who worked in one of the shops, for example, said that men customers 'are always chatting me up . . . but it happens all the time, and you just have to get used to it really, you learn how to cope with it'. Similarly, a woman member of bar staff said 'you don't really have any choice but to cope with it . . . so you just do . . . it's just something we have to do, even if we get upset we can't show it'. The women who worked in the bars in particular stressed the importance of knowing how to deal with the sexualized behaviour of men customers. They said this was because if men 'had a few drinks, things could get aggressive', and so they had to know exactly how to respond.

The ways in which the women spoke of such behaviour from men customers was entirely different from the way they spoke of it from men workers. They were often angry and outraged by the latter, but there was a level of acceptance of customers. Indeed, they were blasé about it and somewhat surprised that I was even bothering to ask questions about this part of their work. This seemed to be connected to the ways in which they viewed (and indeed experienced) this aspect of their work as routine and normal. Dealing with such behaviour by men customers was inevitable and knowing how to deal with it was a skill they quickly developed.

The women staff dealt with being sexualized by men customers by 'laughing it off', or 'playing along with it'. They said the worst thing they could do was to 'get annoyed with [the men], or to 'look angry', or 'not respond' – even if they were feeling annoyed or threatened. To do this would mean the men would just 'carry on bothering us . . . If you play along with it they think they've got what they wanted, so they go'. The strategy these women use to cope with forms of sexualization from men customers is thus to 'enter into' a form of sexual 'exchange', to respond to some extent to sexual jokes, comments and being chatted up. These responses are, for the women, 'part of the job'. In the catering department in such circumstances, women catering assistants would laugh and joke with men customers, but as mentioned before, in a manner aimed at curtailing the interaction. Thus, when one man asked a catering assistant if she wanted to meet him after work, she laughingly said that she was so tired at the end of the day 'she was no good to anyone'. If men commented on aspects of their appearance, the women would often smile and appear flattered, but then would 'take the edge' off the situation by making jokes ('I don't dress like this normally'), or change the subject.

For women in the catering, bars, and retail and marketing departments, sexualized interactions with men customers took place regularly throughout the working day. For the women operatives, however, such interactions were not routine, because they spent most of their time working the children's rides and men customers did not spend much time there. As one of the women explained: 'We don't really get that many men coming into the children's park, it's mostly mums and grannies who are with the children'.

Women workers and 'people' work

The routine sexualization of the majority of women workers at Fun Land provides some very important indicators as to the dynamics of the production of many of the gendered characteristics of work discussed throughout this chapter. Perhaps the most significant is in the manner in which women workers expected and coped with all manner of forms of sexual behaviour from men customers. Both the expectation and the coping were explained by the catering manager, catering assistants and other women workers as being somehow necessary requirements of the job.

Their comments revealed that coping formed a routine feature of working at Fun Land: 'you have to expect it'. For these women there was no choice but to cope with various forms of sexualization – they had to expect and deal with it. Because there was no option, and because this sexualization by men customers was a pervasive feature of Fun Land, coping became 'normal' routine. In other words, anticipating and dealing with sexual innuendoes, verbal advances, comments and sometimes physical advances from men customers was integral to the job. Indeed, dealing with such interactions formed part of the job requirements for women, as was made absolutely clear by the catering manager's 'if they can't handle it, then they're not up to working here'. It was no accident, no chance occurrence, that women workers needed to cope with these situations; it was recognized to be integral to their work.

The question therefore arises as to why women workers had to cope with sexualization to the extent that it was recognized to be part of their job? What is then striking is that the various forms of sexualization of women by both men customers *and men workers* is that they were explicitly related to the forms of internal workplace regulation which operate specifically in relation to women.

For example, in the case of the women bar staff, the bars manager consistently harassed them while requiring them to wear their uniforms 'off the shoulder'. But the wearing of uniforms constituted a condition of employment, and staff had to wear their uniforms in the 'correct' manner or face dismissal. Moreover, Fun Land's departmental managers had the power to decide the form of uniforms for their seasonal workers, including decisions regarding the 'correct' manner in which the uniforms should be worn. So clearly, it was the bars manager himself who decided that the women bar staff should wear gingham dresses, and that the correct way to wear them was 'off the shoulder'. Here, the controls and regulations to which workers are subject and the sexualization of women converge. The 'correct' wearing of their uniforms was a requirement which sexualized the women bar staff. Not only did the requirement mean the bars manager could 'legitimately' pay them sexual attention (by pulling their dresses down into the 'correct' position) because meeting this requirement was 'part of the job', but the requirement also simultaneously sexualized and degraded them. It made them feel they were being defined primarily through the sexualization that the uniform produced, that they were being turned 'into sex-toys'. The uniform requirement thus acted to sexually commodify women workers: to turn them into commercial sex-objects.

This was also evident elsewhere than the bar. Men customers also made comments/innuendoes about how women catering assistants looked sexually attractive in their uniforms. Here again, the form of the uniform – which the women have no choice but to wear – turned them into objects of sexual attention for men. The uniform, and behind that, the requirement to wear the uniform, sexually commodified women.

The links between sexualization and forms of control and regulation of women workers extend far beyond uniforms, however, for most forms of sexualization of women relate to their general personal appearance and men customers and workers made routine comments about the appearance of women workers with clear sexual innuendoes. For instance, men operatives would openly 'judge' whether or not women would be good in bed on the basis of their appearance, and they were always 'eyeing up' women. Women workers' appearance was also the object of attention when they were hassled walking through the park: as reported above, it was 'a tits and bums show'. Men customers also routinely visually objectified women and made reference to their appearance in sexual innuendoes/comments/jokes, to the extent that the women felt 'we were on display for them'.

However, apart from the women operatives, all the women workers at Fun Land required the 'right' appearance to work there. It was a condition of their recruitment and continued employment, and at its centre was visual attractiveness. It was precisely this 'attractive', 'right' appearance which was subject to constant sexual attention from men (both customers and workers). As with the case of uniforms, the conditions and controls which operated in relation to the 'right' appearance for women workers, served to produce a sexually commodified female workforce. This process of commodification took place through 'attractiveness' being systematically prioritized above all other 'requirements' of women workers: they had to fulfil this criterion above all else. This prioritization of sexual attractiveness was embodied in the general manager's comment that women employees: 'ideally . . . should be like Raquel Welch'. Sexual attractiveness was thus part of what was 'sold' to employers by women in 'exchange' for employment.

The conditions and controls which operated in relation to the appearance of women workers operated to sexualize them and to define them primarily in terms of their sexual attractiveness. This reduced their status as workers. The systematic sexualization of women and the conditions and regulations to which they were subject placed them in a situation where they were defined primarily in relation to their sexual attractiveness, and turned them into sexual commodities. These processes prevented women having any choice in relation to this definition (in how they were defined). Being sexually attractive was a condition of both entry into the workplace, and of remaining there. Failure to be sexually attractive (to be a sexual commodity) lead to dismissal, but it meant that the work they did and their skills went largely unnoticed.

This was because the actual work of women became, in part, the work of being and dealing with their location as sexual objects. They had to engage in sexual 'exchanges' initiated by men customers and to give them 'what they wanted'. It was part of their job to engage in forms of sexualized work. When men customers paid women sexual attention, the women to some extent had to 'respond'. They were compelled to laugh, look flattered, smile and enter into it. Women in this position had, in other words, to provide sexual services for men. Men appropriated these forms of work – that is, they got access to these forms of sexual servicing – through the conditions operating in relation to women's employment. They were able to initiate and define the nature of sexual interactions, and they got to feel good about themselves. They had their egos boosted and got sexual thrills. The sexual commodification of women workers therefore produced a sexual power relationship between men customers and women workers.

As with wives working in pubs referred to in Chapter 3, the women workers at Fun Land served, indeed worked, as sexual attractions for men customers. The majority of women at Fun Land were therefore not only 'economically productive' workers – they not only stacked the shelves, served drinks and food, cleared the tables and carried out all manner of other tasks necessary for the production of Fun Land's goods and services – but in addition they provided sexual services for men customers. Moreover, they had to perform this work whenever it was required. It was compulsory if they were to have access to, and retain, employment. The compulsion to perform such work was produced by the requirements of their sexualized employment.

The ways in which part of women's work was structured through this power relation gives substance to some of the characteristics of the gendered organization of work which have emerged from the evidence presented throughout this chapter. The significance of women workers being constructed as 'needing' the right appearance to get a job appeared to lie in women workers being ascribed a particular role in 'people' work or customer relations. But having the right appearance (and the other regulations and controls to which women workers are subject) is intimately connected to the production of a sexually commodified female workforce and the work women do is in part constituted by this location. This suggests that one of women's main roles in customer relations work is the sexual servicing of men customers.

This work is done by women for men customers, and for men customers alone, and yet the language used in relation to customer relations at Fun Land was gender-neutral. This is why it was difficult to make sense of the allocation of a specific role to women in customer relations. Specifically, it was why it was difficult to understand why women needed to have the 'right' appearance 'because of the customers'. It was argued earlier that if this was the case, then presumably men employees should also be subject to similar (or parallel) kinds of conditions and regulations in relation to their appearance to help produce a successful establishment by increasing custom and sales. But in fact this role in customer relations was both gender-specific in terms of employees (it is women who carried it out) and gender-specific in terms of customers (it was done for men customers). Women's role in customer relations was, in other words, not straightforwardly to do with the production of profit, but also to do with the (re)production of gendered power relations.

This set of connections gains further weight when we consider the few women who were employed as operatives. These were women who had the 'wrong' appearance to work in the occupations in which the majority of women were clustered. They were 'too butch' and 'too manly'; they did not fulfil the criteria of being (hetero)sexually attractive. In conditions of labour shortage (as during the 1989 season), such women were employed in the children's park, where men customers did not spend much time: 'It's mostly mums and grannies'. Because these women did not meet the requirements of feminine attractiveness, they were employed in a capacity where this 'failure' to meet the criteria was relatively insignificant, that is where they had minimal contact with men customers. They therefore escaped the requirements of producing and maintaining a sexually attractive appearance (which explains the difference in forms of regulation these women were subject to compared with the other women workers). They did not have to carry out the sexual work which other women had to do routinely, but they were also, though differently, sexually harassed (see below), and in conditions of abundant labour they might not have been employed at all.

Sexual work and men workers

But the sexual power relationship between men and women produced through the conditions operating in relation to most of women's employment at Fun Land was not limited simply to that between women workers and men customers. It also operated between women workers and the men who were employed there. Part of the significance of the definition of women workers as sexualized workers, lies in sets of gendered power relations between men and women workers, for men workers also appropriated their own benefits from women occupying this position. First, men workers (like men customers) appropriated forms of sexual work performed by women. Women workers routinely 'entered into' sexualized interactions initiated by men workers and dealt with these in similar ways to those initiated by men customers. Second, because of women's location as workers, they were in no better position to resist sexualization from men workers than they were to resist it from customers, whether or not dealing with men workers was viewed as 'part of the job'. There was nothing the women could do except 'cope' with the behaviour of the men operatives, much less anything they could do about the bars manager. Third, because women workers at Fun Land were defined primarily as sexualized workers, their status as workers was systematically undermined *vis-à-vis* men workers. Hence, men workers occupied a structurally more powerful position within the workplace than women workers, and they were in a position to dominate the construction of the workplace hierarchy.

Men workers occupied this more powerful position because men and women were different *kinds* of workers at Fun Land. Men did not have to carry out sexual work in the way that women did, and they were not subject to the same forms of exploitation of their work as women. Put simply, men did not have their status as workers undermined by a subordinate sexual status. Women did.

The fact that men and women were different kinds of workers explains why the recruitment requirements for the occupations in which the men were clustered were variable and concerned with specific occupational requirements. Unlike women, men did not need something extra to be employees. Women had *always* to be sexualized workers. This was the main employment criterion in all the jobs they occupied. The systematic prioritization of this requirement meant that if women were not attractive, it did not matter whether or not they could claim any other labour market resources (for example, occupationally specific skills), they simply would not be employed.

Men, in contrast, because their employment position was not subject to any similar or parallel set of processes through which they were defined and located as a group of workers, were able to claim (and be seen to) possess various labour market resources, such as strength or specific occupational 'skills'. Occupations could be defined as the preserve of men by linking the occupations to specific skills and capacities which, in the given circumstances, only men could claim to possess. Thus the work of operating the rides could be claimed to require physical strength, when in fact it only required pushing buttons. Moreover, because they were sexualized, women workers could do little to challenge this situation. Women as women were not able to possess particular occupational skills because the primary labour market resource women were recognized to possess was their value as sexual servicers.

The specific conditions operating in relation to women's employment meant, therefore, that not only did men employees have access to sexual servicing from women employees, but the conditions also meant men were advantaged in their relationship to employment/the workplace. Men catering assistants, for instance, remained workers in this occupation pretty well irrespective of what they did. In sharp contrast, women in this occupation had a highly conditional position as workers. They remained employed only if they maintained their position as sexual subjects and if they carried out sexual work. Thus, within a given occupation, the dynamics of the construction of women as sexual workers meant that men came to occupy a more privileged and powerful position than women. In this case, the dynamics meant that men occupied the position of relatively unconditional (unregulated) workers.

This set of dynamics between men and women is particularly interesting in the case of the small number of women who were employed as operatives. These women occupied a more powerful position than other women workers at Fun Land, in that they did not fulfil the conditions of being sexual workers and therefore did not provide sexual services, and did not have their status as workers undermined through routine sexualization. It would seem therefore that these women would have been better placed to 'compete' (that is, to be more equal) with men workers at Fun Land than the other women. However, they were actually not able to compete with the men workers because they were excluded from the fast rides, and this exclusion took place precisely because they were seen not to be sexually attractive. They could therefore only work in situations where there were no men customers – that is, in the children's park. In other words, the mechanism which excluded women from the fast rides (and thus created the gendered division between the rides) was precisely the 'fact' that these women were only 'qualified' to work in situations away from men customers. The construction of the 'different' occupational requirements of the fast rides and the children's rides was maintained precisely through the employment requirements which operated in relation to the majority of women. Women operatives were denied the ability to compete with men operatives by an internal gender segregation which was produced within the occupation and which itself was based upon the dynamics of the construction of women as sexual workers. Men, therefore, maintained their structurally more powerful position within the workplace.

Men were also active agents in the construction of women as

sexual workers. Men managers participated in the creation of regulations which reduced women's status, and men (across occupations and all the way down the occupational hierarchy) colluded in producing the conditions in which women could be and were routinely sexualized. In other words, men workers were key agents in the construction of women as sexual workers, and they, like the men customers, gained considerable benefits from this. They too got access to forms of sexual servicing, but they also got to occupy a more powerful position in the workplace.

Since men did gain considerable benefits from the construction of women as sexual workers, the women operatives who did not have to possess a sexually attractive appearance and who did not sexually service men, posed a threat to the power that men gained through this construction. These women demonstrated that having an appearance which men find pleasing and providing sexual services which men derive pleasure and power from, is not inevitable for women. This threatened the power that men had over women in the domain of (hetero)sexuality, and hence in the workplace. This may explain why groups of men operatives and the parks manager colluded in physically threatening these women. If the women attempted to resist these threats – by complaining and objecting – they were dismissed. Of course, this also maintained the internal segregation of the occupation, because it kept the few women in it marginalized, reduced their status and 'encouraged' the other women to conform.

Men as workers, men as customers and Fun Land as an employer, all therefore derived considerable benefits from the construction of women as sexual workers. For men workers, it meant they always occupied a more powerful position than women and were able to exploit the position of women within the workplace. For the employers, it meant that women served (in fact worked) as sexual attractions satisfying men customers. And for both men workers and customers, it meant they had access to, and could appropriate sexual servicing from, women workers.

In sum, the conditions which operated in relation to women's employment – having and maintaining an attractive appearance – formed part of the process through which women workers were sexualized, and hence downgraded/degraded. Through these controls and regulations – or the commodification of women's appearance – the status of women created was that of sexualized and subordinate actors. Women could do little to resist this process, as it precisely defined and shaped their position in the workplace. They could only be employees if they were sexual subordinates and carried out sexual work. The routine sexual exploitation of women by men was therefore the result of *work relations which operated only for women.*

These gendered work relations also operated at Global Hotel. The way women workers at Global Hotel as a group were constructed as needing the same qualities to be workers, the manner in which men were systematically exempt from these requirements (and indeed any requirements that constructed men as a unified group of workers), and the way in which women, and only women, had to maintain a particular personal appearance to retain their position as employees, meant that women constituted a different category of workers than men. Women were ascribed a common status as workers, whereas men were not. This common status limited women's ownership of any other labour market resources other than that of attractiveness. Women, therefore, entered both workplaces on a different footing from men. Men and women carried out different sorts of work and women were sexually exploited. This applied even when men and women were nominally located in the same occupations.

Existing studies of service employment relations have also documented the operation of similar gendered work relations. In a whole variety of service jobs, women's employment is conditional upon them fulfilling a specific set of criteria relating to their personal appearance, and such conditions do not operate for men. These studies also suggest that the conditions placed on women are connected to the way in which work they are routinely required to carry out in the labour market is partly sexual work. Woolf (1990), for example, has documented the ways in which women are sexualized in their employment situations precisely because they comply to appearance requirements which operate in relation to their employment. Women employees are, for instance, sexually objectified by employers precisely because they comply with a dress code which specifies short skirts, clinging blouses, high heels and make-up. Moreover, women must deal with this routine sexualization if they are to retain their employment position. If they do not enter into sexual exchanges, and make men feel good through sexual banter, their status as workers is threatened.

To return to the example of the airline industry, women flight attendants routinely cope with men customers flirting and propositioning them (Hochschild 1983; Williams 1988). One airline executive confirmed the sexual nature of the flight attendant's work when he said, 'You [men passengers] would get a kick if a hostess grinned at you. It was as if she had spent the night with you' (Williams 1988: 95). But this is not just clean innocent fun. For if women flight attendants do not respond, if they do not smile and enter in sexual 'exchanges' with men, like the women at Fun Land and Global Hotel, their employment position is under threat. As one flight attendant said, 'the minute you don't smile you get a complaint' (Williams 1988: 107).

The sexualized nature of women's work means that even when men and women work in the same occupation – be it behind a bar or in a restaurant, as a flight attendant or a bank clerk or a secretary – men and women are different sorts of workers. Women, as well as men, must serve food and drinks to customers, and take in and give out cheques or type letters, and wear clean company uniforms or 'appropriate' clothes. But women and only women must maintain an attractive, appealing appearance, smile, make customers feel good and respond to sexual advances and innuendoes. The sexual subordinate status of women is not, however, simply operative between women workers and men customers, but also operates between women and men workers. Commenting on the location of women in relation to men flight attendants, one woman observed, 'we are pets with sex thrown in, sweet but we can be used'; while another said, 'you are like some kind of social property' (Williams 1988: 130).

Given the sexual content of women's labour and the particular forms of exploitation of women's work, the fact that men and only men can be promoted to senior flight stewards in the airline industry (Williams 1988), or that their career paths are radically different in banking (Llewellyn 1981), must be viewed not simply as the outcome of men controlling women's ungendered labour and women's access to labour market resources, but rather as the outcome of a patriarchal construction of wage-labour relations and labour market resources themselves. As Williams (1988: 131) observed:

women were doing ... different kinds of work to the men
next to them ... The women were expected to smile at the
[customers] as they entered ... and 'assist' the male [workers].
But the men alone could work in the higher grades of the
occupation ... [but] the work was similar except in the case
of the 'emotion labour' carried out by the women who were
expected to [be] attractive and desirable young women.

Sexual work and women's employment

Sexual work relations operating for women are hardly specific to
Fun Land and Global Hotel. Given the way in which all manner of
service jobs routinely sexualize women's work, and the ways in
which women are routinely located as constituting different sort of
workers compared with men through this sexualization, it seems
that the specific conditions attached to women's employment
uncovered at these two worksites, far from being atypical, may be
one of the constitutive features of 'women's work'. Indeed, even
studies of women's manufacturing or professional employment
suggest similar processes are in operation. For instance, in her study
of semi-skilled manual workers in an engineering firm, Purcell
found that interactions between men and women workers were
often sexualized (in the form, for instance, of flirting), that men
usually initiated such interactions, and that women workers were
'forced to respond according to a prescribed pattern' (Purcell 1991:
143). In such situations, women played along with the jokes, the
innuendoes and sometimes physical attention from men (such as
knee squeezing and hugging), and 'responded with warmth or at
least wit' (ibid.). This was, moreover, the only successful response
the women could deploy. If they did not 'go along with it', they
were 'subjected to increasingly hostile teasing and personal
criticism' (ibid.). Similar accounts of 'joking' sexualization have
been provided from school staff rooms and classrooms (Cunnison
1989), advertising agencies (Gregory 1987), retailing companies
(Cockburn 1991) and hospitals (Bradley 1989) It seems, therefore,
that the compulsion on women to carry out various forms of
sexual work in employment situations may extend well outside of
tourism and the commercial services sector.

The suggestion that women are routinely compelled to carry

out forms of sexual labour in the context of employment, raises all sorts of issues regarding the gendering of the labour market, and in particular for our understandings of service work. Hence, the gendered structuring of work relations identified at Fun Land and Global Hotel uncovers a number of issues for the feminist analyses of the gendering of the labour market discussed in Chapter 2. The next and final chapter therefore turns to a discussion of the significance of sexual work relations, as well as family work relations, for the contemporary labour market as a whole.

Note

1 Rather than focusing on one particular occupation or set of occupations, and changes over time and across different worksites – as has been typical of recent empirical work on the gendered operations of the labour market (e.g. Bradley 1989; Crompton and Sanderson 1990) – it was decided to carry out fieldwork on the whole range of different occupations to be found within individual workplaces. That is, in-depth fieldwork within specific leisure operations was to form the basis of the research. This allowed exploration of both the general hypothesis that sexuality may structure gendered work relations within employment, and the specific research questions formulated through the existing literature. Various factors and workplace processes, which might potentially act to shape work relations between men and women, could then be explored – from control of workers to the role of customers.

5

The condition of women's work

The material presented in the previous four chapters has shown that far from existing only outside the domain of employment, both family and sexual work relations can play a significant role in structuring gendered work relations within the labour market.

In the case of management in hotel and catering, the work relations (or relations of production) within the occupation were shown to be frequently organized by the patriarchal relations of the family. Despite wives being included within the contracts of managers of many establishments (they were hired as part of a married management 'team'), their husbands directly controlled and appropriated the women's occupational work, and some of these benefits were then creamed off by the men's employers. Wives had no wage–labour agreement (or labour contract) with the companies who employed 'them'. They were not waged employees; rather, they worked within the occupation for their hubands, who had direct control over their labour and decided on the form of their wives' remuneration. The contract under which the wives worked within the occupation was the marriage contract. The specific gendered work relations governing much of hotel and catering management are thus family work relations, or the family mode of production. The forms of control and exploitation to which wives are subject within this occupation centre around the manner in which work or production is organized in the patriarchal family.

At the hotel and leisure park, the forms of control and exploitation to which women employees were subject were also an outcome of the manner in which production was organized, but in these cases it was a question of patriarchal structuring of waged-labour. For women to have access to employment, most had no choice but to occupy the position of sexual subjects. To get a job, most women (regardless of their occupation) were required to fulfil conditions which related to the production of an 'attractive' female workforce. These conditions meant (as was shown in particular for the leisure park) that the primary work of women was the work of being a sexual commodity, and they did this on top of serving drinks or making sandwiches or washing up. Expecting and dealing with forms of sexual objectification from men customers and men co-workers was an integral part of their work and they were defined, indeed were only usually allowed into the workplace, as sexual workers. Sexual exploitation in the workplace was the outcome of work relations which operated only for women: only women had to fulfil the conditions of being a sex-worker and carry out sexual work in order to be workers – to exchange their labour in the marketplace.

Gendered work and the control of women's labour in the labour market

Recognizing this structuring by gender of work relations at the two tourist organizations and within the occupation of hotel and catering management has important implications for feminist labour market theory. Such sets of work relations have not previously been recognized to exist within contemporary employment.

In Chapters 2 and 3, for example, it was shown that when attempts are made to explicitly locate the forms of control of women's labour operating in the labour market (in particular, the accounts of Hartmann 1979, 1981; Walby 1986, 1990), the major, indeed the only, form of control is seen to be control of women's access to jobs and wages (through exclusion and segregation). In these accounts, the subsequent gender division of labour in the labour market results from this control, and in particular, segregation of occupations reproduces gender divisions. Attaching this degree of significance to the control of women's access to wages and to occupational segregation derives from an assumption within such analyses that the labour market is an entity whose actual structure is created by the (ungendered) relations of capitalism. More specifically, they assume that capital produces jobs (the places in a hierarchy of waged-workers within the labour market), while (on top of this) the patriarchal control of women's labour limits women's access to these jobs.

The evidence presented in relation to hotel and pub managers and the tourist workplaces challenges these assumptions. As was shown in Chapter 3, the sets of work relations based upon the patriarchal structure of the family and the direct control of women's labour by manager-husbands simply cannot be account- ed for within such analyses. It challenges the assumptions which derive from the definition of the labour market structure as wholly determined by the relations of capital; that is, that the only form of work taking place within the context of the labour market is waged work, and that the only form of control of women's labour operating within this sphere operates to limit women's access to waged work. Women who work as part of married management 'teams' do unpaid work, and the control of this labour in this context is not directly due to the exclusion of women from, or their segregation within, the labour market.[1] The sets of work relations between men and women within the labour market cannot, therefore, be reduced to patriarchal control of access to wage-labour.

Similarly, the mode of control of women employed in tourism also problematizes such analyses. Rather than exclusionary control of women's access to jobs and wages, the control of women's labour in the two worksites studied has been seen to centre around sexuality – around the ways in which it is compulsory for women to be sexual workers.

What is perhaps of greatest significance in terms of the evidence presented from Fun Land, Global Hotel and hotel and catering establisment management, is that rather than the labour market being structured by ungendered economic relations, the 'economic' itself has been shown to be gendered. Rather than capital producing the places in an (ungendered) hierarchy of workers, on top of which patriarchal relations operate to determine who fills what places (by men organizing to control and limit women's access to wages), the hierarchy itself has been shown to be gendered in the first instance: it is intrinsically structured by patriarchal social relations.

At the two tourist workplaces, the labour market was shown to be gendered *prior* to occupations being differentiated. Specifically, women workers had to fulfil the conditions of being sexualized workers *regardless* of their occupation. Men and women were constituted as different kinds of workers within these workplaces, *even when they were located in the same jobs*. To be workers, women had to be 'attractive' workers and carry out forms of sexualized work, whereas men did not have to do this. Thus, as was made clear in Chapter 4, women not only took orders, served food and drinks and cleared tables, they (and only they) also provided sexual servicing for men, both customers and co-workers. Women were thus not only 'economically productive' but also 'sexually productive' workers. The fact that it was only women who were required to carry out such sexual servicing as a condition of their employment shows that men and women participated in the two workplaces within substantially different relations of production. Production practices are therefore gendered. In addition, this gendered production has been shown not merely to be an outcome of some sort of distanced 'logic of capital', but also to be created by the direct actions of men – managers and co-workers. At Fun Land, for instance, it was shown that both groups of men actively engaged in producing the sets of conditions and the forms of regulation that meant that if women wanted to be workers, they were required to occupy the position of sex-objects and engage in forms of sexual work or sexual production.

Husbands and wives who are employed as married managers of hotel and catering establishments also participate in this occupation within different relations of production. Men work within the occupation as employees in the context of a direct capital–labour contract with hotel and catering companies, whereas women work in the context of a marital relationship with their husbands, with no direct capital–labour relation. They work as wives rather than waged labourers.

In both cases, the relations of production in which women participated meant that their status as workers in relation to men within the sphere of employment was denigrated. Women were placed in a relatively powerless position, in that these forms of production (that is, family and sexualized employment) carried with them, and indeed were based upon, specific forms of control and appropriation of women's labour or work. In the case of wives in hotel and pub management, husbands directly controlled and appropriated their labour; and in the case of women workers at Global Hotel and Fun Land, women's position as sexual workers meant their sexual/people work was routinely appropriated by men. Indeed, the manner in which production was organized at the two tourist workplaces meant that this exploitation of sexual work was 'part of the job'.

Thus both the forms of work women carry out (unpaid family work and sexual wage work), and the conditions under which they carry them out, centre around the ways in which production itself is gendered. This gendering of production means that men and women within the two workplaces, and in the other occupations considered in this book, *are different sorts of workers*. They do different sorts of work even when working alongside each other, and have different relationships of and to production. Moreover, the gendering of production means that men occupy a structurally more powerful position in all these various areas of employment, a position from which they can control and appropriate some of the products of the work of women.

The ways in which production has been shown to be gendered, and the implications of this gendering – in particular, the forms of control and appropriation operating in relation to women waged-workers – clearly problematize those accounts of the gendered operation of the labour market which suggest that the 'economic' or 'production' are ungendered products of capitalist relations. Such accounts assume the only form of work which takes place in the labour market is that carried out in relation to this ungendered structure; that is, paid work which produces goods and services *for capital*. But in fact production is both gendered and is a product of the patriarchal actions of men, and it involves men and women carrying out different sorts of work in different sets of conditions, and men workers deriving some benefit from their women co-workers.

Because men and women in the areas of employment considered in this book work within different relations of production, this also problematizes the account of the consequences of gendered occupational segregation within the labour market put forward by Hartmann (1979) and Walby (1986, 1990). As was shown in Chapter 2, both authors assume that gendered occupational segregation and men's power over women in the labour market are created out of men's control of women's access to jobs and wages, and that this control equals the creation of gender. But the gendered organization of work relations considered in this book suggest that rather than being created out of control of access to jobs and wages, gender relations in the labour market (including gender segregation itself) are an outcome of the different sorts of work relations of men and women – that is, the way in which men and women are different sorts of workers in the labour market.

At Fun Land and Global Hotel, women's relation to men was structured by men's power because of the manner in which production was gendered in terms of sexual work relations. Men were more powerful than women in this context because to be a woman at these two worksites was to be a sexual worker and to be subject to the appropriation of sexual labour. Similarly, in the case of married managers of hotel and catering establishments, the social production of gender (of men and women) was not simply related to the control of women's access to wages. Rather, the relation between men and women, or the social meaning of gender within this occupation, was an outcome of the ways in which production was organized in terms of the patriarchal family (or to put it simply, marriage), where husbands directly control and appropriate the work of wives. All these cases suggest that an explanation of the division of labour between men and women in terms of waged work, produced by men's control of women's access to wages, cannot adequately account for the social construction of gender relations.

Gendered workers and patriarchal capitalism

In addition to problematizing the view that the control of access to jobs and wages constitutes gender, the ways in which production has been revealed to be organized in terms of family and sexual work relations also supports and develops the view (discussed in Chapter 2) that capitalism is patriarchally constituted. A number of analyses have been considered which locate 'the worker' as gendered. In particular, a range of research and analyses have shown that the non-ownership and appropriation of women's labour in the family means that women are not as 'free' to exchange their labour with employers as men. It was also shown that this gendering of 'the worker' has led a number of feminist commentators (especially Joan Acker and Carol Pateman) to view the labour market not simply as a distinct, capitalist structure, but as an intrinsically gendered formation. They are therefore critical of 'dual systems' approaches, where patriarchy and capitalism are held as two separate, yet interrelating, sets of social relations.

The material presented in this book clearly supports the view that 'capitalism' is gendered. In particular, the location of women as unpaid family and sexual workers in the labour market shows that in addition to the appropriation of women's labour in the family, women are not 'workers' in the same way as men because of the patriarchal structuring of labour market production itself. Thus, while women in the tourist workplaces had to carry out 'extra' sexual work and were subject to the appropriation of their sexual labour, women in hotel and pub management were not workers in the same way as men because they were not free to exchange their labour at all: they worked as wives rather than as waged–workers.

These instances of the ways in which women are not 'workers' on the same terms as men supports Acker's (1989) view that the ability to freely exchange labour for a wage is not universal within modernity. Moreover, it suggests, as was discussed in Chapter 2, that the labour market is far more fundamentally gendered than the 'dual systems' approaches suggest. Specifically, it shows how women's disadvantage in the labour market is not simply an outcome of the control of their access to jobs and wages, but also that participation in employment for women involves particular forms of sexual and unpaid appropriation of labour – to which men are not subjected. Thus, not only is the ability to 'exchange' labour gendered, but also the constitution of 'labour power' is different for men and women.

To date, only a few feminist commentators have raised the possibility that labour market economic processes, including production, may be gendered. Beechey (1988), for example, has called for analyses which consider the manner in which gender may contribute to, or be embodied in, labour market production. However, she herself did not attempt to specify how, or in what ways, such gendering may be intrinsic to production. Similarly, Scott (1986) has argued that in labour market (and social stratification) theory, attention needs to be turned to analyses of the ways in which economic processes may be gendered. She puts forward the hypothesis that the continued assumption that economic processes are gender-neutral, seriously undermines understandings of the mechanisms of gender inequality.

The material presented throughout this book certainly supports such views. In particular, it has shown how the assumption that the economic is gender-neutral precludes analysis of the ways in which men and women may work within different relations of production in the labour market and, therefore, how it limits understandings of the gendering of the labour market itself.

Sexuality and employment

The effects of this limiting assumption are perhaps most clear in terms of sexuality. As was clear in the discussion of feminist analyses of the labour market in Chapter 2, sexuality and (the assumed to be ungendered) economic relations have been consistently separated. Sexuality has rarely been considered in terms of economic forms. Moreover, feminist labour market theorists have repeatedly failed to get to grips with the significance of sexuality as a constituent of gender in the labour market. Indeed, it was suggested that these are enduring features of feminist analyses of the labour market, even of the more recent studies which have explicitly focused on sexuality and employment. For example, while Pringle's and Cockburn's recent studies show sexuality permeating the workplace – workplace life is thoroughly sexualized – they nevertheless fail to show how sexuality relates to the production of men's economic and other advantages in the labour market. That is to say, they fail to show the significance of sexuality in terms of the gendering of the labour market itself. Chapter 2, for example, showed that although Cockburn discusses the exploitation of women's sexuality in the workplace, this exploitation is only seen as significant in terms of (gender-neutral) capitalist production: she sees only such work as being extorted for profit. The possibility that the appropriation of sexuality in the labour market may be gendered, or that such an appropriation of sexuality may contribute to the construction of power relations between men and women workers, is not considered. That is, the only form of production that she recognizes as taking place in the labour market is (gender-neutral) capitalist production.

The material presented in this book suggests, however, that sexual work and the appropriation of sexuality is not simply connected to the forces of capitalist production, but that such work and appropriation is gendered. Thus, it is not only capital, but also men (customers and co-workers) who benefit from women's sexual work. Moreover, it has been shown how the organization of production in terms of sexuality may be key in terms of power relations beween men and women in the labour market: for the production of men's advantage over women in the labour workplace. Thus, for example, it has been shown how the location of women as sexual workers in tourism, limits their ownership of any labour market resources other than their value as sexual servicers. Men, on the other hand, because they are not constructed as a unified group of workers, are able to claim to possess a range of occupational resources (such as specific skills and capacities). In sum, the material presented in this book shows that Cockburn's location of the economic as gender-neutral leads to an under-estimation of the significance sexuality can play in terms of the gendering of the labour market.

It will also be recalled how, in Pringle's analysis, where she documents the discursive and symbolic construction of sexualized workplace identities, the relationship between sexual identities and the gendering of the labour market was not addressed. Thus, for example, she did not show how men's symbolic and cultural power over women produces men's power to appropriate women's labour. The material presented in this book, however, challenges the assumption that sexuality and gender are cultural products which are quite separate from economic relations. It has shown, for example, that both sexuality and gender may be actively produced through (gendered) relations of production, and that men's power to appropriate and control women's labour may be effected through such gendering of the relations of production in terms of sexuality. Thus, the relations of sexual production have been shown to locate women in a position of sexual servicers, and to give men power to access and appropriate women's sexual labour.

Workplace sexual identities may thus be seen to be constituted in relations of appropriation (Adkins and Lury 1994). For example, women producing and maintaining a sexualized identity is both required and appropriated. Presenting a certain appearance and a sexualized way of being (or sexual 'self') is part of their job. For women, their (sexual) 'selves' are produced through the relations of production and subject to appropriation. Men, on the other hand, are not required to produce and maintain a particular sexual 'self' as part of their jobs and their sexual 'selves' are not the subject of appropriation. Clearly, rather than being cultural and symbolic formations quite separate from economic relations (cf. Pringle), sexual workplace identities may be achieved through workplace practices themselves (gendered relations of production and appropriation). Moreover, the relations of sexual production and appropriation significantly structure men's power over women in the labour market. Thus, Pringle's assumption that the economic is irrelevant to the formation of sexuality and gender in the labour market obscures the significance of sexuality in terms of the construction of men's power over women in the labour market.

Cockburn's and Pringle's assumptions that sexuality is differentiated from economic relations and that the economic is gender-neutral, not only leads them into a position where they downplay the significance of sexuality in terms of the general structuring force of gender in the labour market, but also leads them to adopt a limited view of the social structuring of sexuality itself in the workplace. In Chapter 2, it was shown that both Cockburn and Pringle distinguish between coercive and non-coercive heterosexuality for women in the labour market. Both see coercive heterosexuality as a problem, but they view non-coercive heterosexuality as affording women pleasure and agency. Non-coercive heterosexuality may be disconnected from men's power over women and, indeed, may even be used as a threat to men's advantage in the workplace.

This understanding of sexuality is, however, problematized by the material presented here. In particular, the ways in which both 'coercive' and 'non-coercive' heterosexuality have been shown to be structured by men's power over women in the tourist organizations, raises questions about Pringle's and Cockburn's differentiation of the two. In the two tourist workplaces, work itself was sexual for women. Dealing with sexualization from men customers and men co-workers was part of the job. The gendering of production in this way placed women in a position where they were consistently sexually objectified and used by men. The relations of production therefore produced, or contributed to the production of, a form of sexuality which was structured in term's of men's dominance.

At the hotel and leisure park, women did in fact enjoy some of their sexualized interactions with men, and found most of them annoying rather than threatening. In addition, the majority of women were not literally forced to conform to the conditions attached to their employment – they did it readily. But this is not to say that engaging in sexual interactions with men was not compulsory, nor that these interactions were not structured by men's power. The conditions attached to women's employment meant that these interactions were compulsory and men did have more power within them. Resistance to this situation by refusing to 'exchange' sexual labour, or resisting sexual commodification, led to dismissal, or to men escalating the interaction and getting nasty. Resistance was therefore possible, but it carried a high social cost. In most sexualized interactions with men, women therefore gave the men 'what they wanted'. But this was not a straightforward case of women welcoming men's attention or responding to advances because women thought men deserved the flattery or because they wanted to establish a relationship. Men had power to initiate and determine the form of their interactions with women and women *had* to respond.

Thus both coercive and non-coercive – even pleasurable – sexual interactions between men and women were structured by the same power relations. The sexualized interactions did not fall into different categories and types – they were the same basic social relationships played with variations. Work relations at the hotel and leisure park demonstrate that men's power in sexual relations is socially produced, and that it is maintained through, *inter alia*, the way sexual exploitation is structured at the point of production. They also show that the exploitation of women within heterosexual relations is not simply associated with particular forms of heterosexual practice, still less is it associated with particular sorts of men; rather, work relations are one of the elements constituting heterosexual relations (Adkins 1992b: 225). In assuming that economic relations are gender-neutral, both Pringle and Cockburn produce a limited view of the social structuring of sexuality (and gender) in the labour market, and in particular they exclude the importance of (gendered) work relations and relations of appropriation in the structuring of both 'coercive' and 'non-coercive' heterosexuality in terms of men's power. They are therefore led to produce an over-voluntaristic account of labour market sexuality (Adkins and Lury 1994).

In Chapter 2, it was shown that the separation between the sexual and the economic is not, however, simply at play in analyses of the labour market. It is also a dominant assumption in analyses of the sexual harassment of women at work. Here, the labour market is defined primarily as an economic entity, while sexual harassment is defined as non-economic. Thus in MacKinnon's (and most of Stanko's) analyses, there is an assumption that sexual harassment is imposed on top of the economic formation of the labour market. But far from constituting non-economic relations which are played out on top of an already structured labour market, the evidence presented in Chapter 4 has shown that sexuality constitutes part of the (gendered) 'economic' itself. Thus sexuality is embedded within, and organizes, production.

The way in which sexuality has been shown to organize production also problematizes the implicit assumption found in MacKinnon's (1979) (and most of Stanko's) analyses that sexuality in the labour market is synonymous with practices of sexual harassment which act simply to reinforce or maintain economic divisions between men and women within the sphere of employment. This book has shown that sexuality may, in contrast, actively contribute to the *production* of economic divisions between men and women. Thus we have seen, for example, how the compulsion on women to carry out sexual work locates men as a more powerful group of workers. Moreover, it is also clear that this is an outcome of the way in which sexuality in the labour market is not synonymous with 'harassment' (as is implied at times by Stanko 1988), but exists as a pervasive 'economic' relation between men and women. Men are constructed both as a more powerful group of workers than women, and as having power to harass, sexualize and appropriate women's sexual labour, because of the gendered relations of production. Thus, the material presented here suggests that rather than being an intrusion into the workplace and unrelated to labour market practices, the sexual harassment and sexualization of women at work is deeply embedded in such practices. Specifically, it suggests that sexual harassment and the sexualization of women is the *outcome* of the organization of (gendered) relations of production.

Heterosexuality and the control and appropriation of women's labour

The organization of work relations between men and women uncovered in these tourist workplaces thus clearly have important implications for the development of our understanding of the gendering of the labour market. But, in addition, they are also significant in terms of our understanding of sexuality. In particular, they have important implications for the analyses of heterosexuality discussed in Chapter 2. One of the most important contributions is the demonstration of how the organization of production in service workplaces actively creates (or contributes to) a form of sexuality which is structured in terms of men's dominance. Thus, the conditions surrounding women's employment at the two workplaces, and within the variety of service jobs considered, can be seen as part of the process through which heterosexuality is made compulsory for women (Rich 1983). At both of the tourist workplaces, being heterosexually available constituted both a condition of work for women and determined the kinds of work they had to carry out: women literally had to work heterosexually (Adkins 1992b: 224). Work relations for women meant they had no choice but to be 'heterosexualized' (Wittig 1982, 1989).

This situation throws light on some of the questions raised by the analyses of heterosexuality discussed in Chapter 2. Some of this work (e.g. Rich 1983; Raymond 1986) asserts that heterosexuality constitutes a set of social relations through which men's economic power and other forms of power over women is produced. Thus heterosexuality is defined as producing men's power to control and appropriate women's (paid and unpaid) labour. Indeed, it was shown that some analysts argue that heterosexuality produces the totality of gender relations (e.g. MacKinnon 1987, 1989). However, none of these analyses actually explicate the connections between the construction of men's economic power over women and heterosexuality – they simply assume them. They do not, for example, suggest how the compulsion on women to be heterosexual provides the conditions through which men can control and appropriate their labour.

Evidence from the two tourist workplaces has shown, however, that there is indeed an important connection between heterosexuality and the control and exploitation of women's labour. The conditions surrounding much of women's service employment – namely, that women must occupy the position of sexually commodified labour to have access to employment – gives men (employers, men workers and men customers) control of, access to and the use of women's labour. The evidence presented in this book therefore suggests that heterosexuality may contribute to the conditions through which women's labour is appropriated by men because of the ways in which labour or work itself may be sexualized for women. Thus it suggests that one of the elements which contributes to the institution of heterosexuality is gendered work relations.

But while heterosexuality has been shown to be connected to the control and appropriation of women's labour, in that part of women's work in the tourist organizations has been shown to be sexual, the evidence presented from the two workplaces does not support the view that gender is always sexualized (MacKinnon, 1987, 1989). For while the organization of work relations, and in particular the conditions surrounding women's employment in the hotel and leisure park, gave men sexual power over women (the power to appropriate forms of sexual servicing), they also afforded men greater access to labour market resources (such as specific occupational skills) and workplace status. Similarly, in the case of husbands and wives in hotel and pub management, while part of the benefits husbands and men customers dervived from the relations of family production took the form of sexualized labour, this did not by any means constitute the only benefit husbands got from the use of their wives' labour. Wives worked not only as sexual attractions for husbands and companies in the pubs and hotels, they also did all the tasks their husbands could not do, or did not want to do. In this context, gender did not just involve the appropriation of sexual work; it also involved the appropriation of straightforwardly occupational work, such as cooking food for sale or doing the books, and domestic work such as washing socks and caring for children (not to mention the emotional work they did which was directly appropriated by husbands; see Delphy and Leonard 1992).

'Sex-work' and gender

While it is clear that gender is not always sexualized, the set of connections that have been uncovered between heterosexuality and the appropriation of women's labour nevertheless also shed light on the issue (discussed in Chapter 2) of the possible links between women's situation in the sex industry and the situation of women who are waged workers outside the sex industry. As was shown earlier, feminist labour market theorists tend to ignore the sex industry and treat it as if it is not part of the 'real' labour market. But other feminists have argued that there are common elements in the situation of women in the sex industry and women 'outside' it. Guillaumin (1981), for example, has argued that marriage and prostitution are linked, in that both are instances of the physical (including sexual) appropriation of women by men, which is possible because women do not own their bodies in the same way as men.

The material from the two workplaces considered in this book suggests that in terms of women's waged-work, there are indeed some important connections between the material situation of women 'sex-workers' and women 'employees'. In particular, the ways in which women at the two tourist workplaces and in the other typical women's service jobs are obliged to carry out sexual labour as a routine part of their job, suggests that the sexual servicing of men may not be specific to the 'sex industry', but rather is a common feature of women's waged-work. The women workers considered in this book were not exchanging sexual intercourse with men for money.[2] But by responding to sexual innuendoes and men's advances – by smiling, looking flattered and entering into it – they were, nevertheless, sexually servicing men. And many prostitutes spend much of their time massaging egos, as well as bodies, and playing 'naughty' games (McLeod 1982; Jarvinen 1993). Moreover, the material presented in this book suggests that this sexual servicing and the appropriation of women's sexual labour in the labour market by men is effected through the ways in which relations of production are themselves gendered. It is the conditions attached to the exchange of women's labour which both compel women to carry out sexual labour and make the appropriation of this labour possible.

Thus, in terms of Guillaumin's analysis, we can see that, as in the cases of marriage and prostitution, in a range of typical women's service jobs the conditions attached to employment mean that women do not own or have as full control over their bodies as men. To be able to gain employment – that is, to exchange their labour – women have to forfeit or at least limit their ability to determine the use of their bodies. They agree to be sexual commodities for use by men. Men's bodies were not the subject of such objectification and appropriation, and so men could be said to 'own' their bodies in a way that women simply do not. In other words, women's limited control of their bodies, which Guillaumin defines at the key condition for the appropriation of women's sexual labour in prostitution and marriage, clearly also operates in women's employment 'outside' the sex industry. Indeed, women's limited ownership of their bodies in the context of service employment relations, through bodily commodification, clearly constitutes a way in which women are not 'workers' in the same way as men, in that it shows, once again, that the conditions attached to the exchange of labour power in tourist service jobs are quite different for men and women (Mies 1986; Pateman 1988; Acker 1990; Cockburn 1991).

But while the material in this book helps to unravel the connections between women sex-workers and women employees in terms of a common appropriation of sexual labour and their limited ownership of their bodies, it also problematizes the view (discussed in Chapter 2) that the use of the term 'sex-work' to describe women's work situation in the sex industry should be abandoned because it (supposedly) obscures the exploitation of women's sexuality in the sex industry through an over-emphasis on the 'free' exchange of sexual services for money. Rather, it shows that this argument (ironically) downplays the extent of sexual exploitation of women by obscuring the ways in which such exploitation is actually also effected through the organization of non-sex-industry, 'ordinary', gendered work relations. This view is problematic because it accepts unquestionably that there can be ungendered exchange. While women's sexuality is certainly exploited in service jobs, this exploitation is the outcome of the different conditions attached to men's and women's employment. In these circumstances, the exchange of women's labour involves a sexual appropriation, while the exchange of men's labour does not. In other words, the exchange of sexual services in return for wages is not 'free' for women. On the contrary, it is a condition of their employment. The argument that the notion of 'sex-work' should be abandoned, therefore, rests on a universalist (liberal) understanding of exchange,[3] where the ability to exchange labour is assumed to be equally available to men and women, and where the conditions of exchange are assumed to be ungendered. Rather than it being a political expedient for feminism to abandon the notion of sex-work, the material presented in this book suggests that this term is important because it exposes common material conditions (forms of appropriation) in women's lives. That is to say, it reveals important aspects of the current organization of women's oppression in western societies.[4]

Gendered work and service labour

The description and analysis of gendered work relations in service jobs offered in this book also has important implications for our understanding of tourist and service work more generally. In Chapter 1, it was shown that tourism is now the subject of some considerable attention, not least because of its perceived significance in national and global economies, and because of general concerns about deindustrialization; the apparent growth of the service sector; the importance of leisure, consumption and consumption practices for social formations; and transformations within 'late' capitalist societies. These concerns were in turn shown to have produced an interest in the specificity of service labour, that is in how service work differs from other forms of wage-labour relations.

Two distinctive analyses of service work were discussed in Chapter 1, those of Offe (1985) and Urry (1990). Both agree that 'service labour' cannot simply be understood in terms of economic relations. Thus, for example, Offe (1985) argues that unlike other forms of waged-labour, service labour involves the (re)production of normal social conditions (the social structure) through a mediation between service providers and service consumers. Urry also stresses the importance of the interaction between service providers and consumers, but in this case the spatial and temporal proximity of production and consumption in tourism are seen to imply that work relations are significantly culturally developed. In particular, he argues that the quality of the interaction between consumers and front-line producers (including the gender, age and race of service providers) becomes part of what is sold (part of the product). Consumer expectations regarding service delivery may thus significantly structure the organization of work relations in tourism and front-line employees may be subject to intervention in terms of their appearance and behaviour, and be specifically trained to deal with the needs of customers. On this basis, Urry suggests, it is no surprise that women are clustered in front-line service jobs.

While Offe's and Urry's analyses certainly make some important suggestions about the specificity of service work, the analysis of tourist service work presented in this book shows that both analyses are limited. They do not address the significance of gender in the specificity of service work. In terms of Offe's analysis, for example, while the forms of service work considered here certainly support his view that the 'mediation' or interaction between producers and consumers is an important characteristic of service labour, they also show that it is *women's sexual labour* rather than men's labour which is implicated in this mediation, and that such 'mediation' takes place through the appropriation of sexual labour. Moreover, if we take his argument that the mediation involved in service labour is important because it creates (or contributes to the production) of 'normal' social conditions, then what is clearly shown by these data is how service labour contributes to reaffirming for men their rights of sexual access to women.

As regards Urry's analysis, while the material presented has certainly shown that the quality or type of interaction between producers and consumers is part of what is 'sold' by employers in tourism, and while the appearance, dress and behaviour of employees has been confirmed to be subject to intense regulation, the clustering of women in front-line jobs and the specific conditions and regulations attached to *their* labour would seem to have more to do with the ways in which production itself (or the economic sphere) is gendered in terms of sexual relations, rather than being the result of consumer expectations or demands existing outside the labour market. This is clear in the way in which men employees are excluded from the kinds of customer relations (sexual) work which women are obliged to carry out as a condition of employment, even when men are located in the same front-line jobs. It is also made clear by the way men front-line employees are excluded from the forms of regulation of their appearance, dress and behaviour to which women were subjected. Some of Urry's analysis is therefore put in question, in that the data presented here problematize his assumption that consumer cultural expectations structure the organization of 'service work', and because they show that his analysis does not recognize the gendered structuring of tourist service work.

In Chapter 4, we saw that the sexual servicing women are required to render is not just a condition of their jobs in the tourist industry, but also a condition of their employment in a variety of service work. In addition, evidence in Chapter 3 suggested that the appropriation of sexual labour also takes place in relation to wives working in hotel and catering establishments: that part of the work of wives in married management 'teams' is constituted by sexual labour – they are 'sexual attractions' within pubs. This suggests that, for women, carrying out forms of sexual work and working as sexual commodities may cut across different occupations and sets of gendered work relations within the sphere of employment. Moreover, given the significance of tourism and the service sector generally for women's employment (see Chapter 1), and the overlap between women's work and service work (both paid and unpaid), the evidence presented in this book suggests that sexual work may be one of the constitutive elements of commercial service work for women.

One further element of the sexual labour carried out by women which has been documented in this book remains to be addressed, namely its racialization. In Chapter 1, research by Phizacklea (1988a) on economic restructuring in Britain was discussed, and in particular her suggestion that an important dimension of the growth of private consumer services, and such expanding areas of women's work as those contributing to Britain's tourist industry, was that in general black women were excluded from them. It was also pointed out that all of the women in the two tourist organizations discussed in this book were white. While the district in which both the hotel and leisure park were located had overwhelmingly white populations, the complete absence of black women workers from the two workplaces does suggest that the conditions surrounding women's employment in commercial services may be significantly racialized. In addition, the evidence presented in this book about the ways in which sexual labour is a common requirement in such service work, suggest that one aspect of the exclusion of black women from this expanding area of women's employment is the racial structuring of sexuality. That is to say, production in commercial services may require entirely 'white' as well as gendered sexual labour.[5] Thus while white women may only be able to exchange their labour if they are sexually commodified and if they carry out sexual labour, black women may not be able to exchange their labour at all. Clearly, this is a tentative suggestion. Further research is required to investigate the ways in which the relations of gendered production and appropriation may be organized in terms of 'whiteness' in the commercial services sector.

Further research is also required to establish the relative significance of both sexual employment relations and family production (as well as other possible gendered relations of production, such as caring employment relations; see Chapter 3) for women's general position within the sphere of employment (both inside and outside the service sector). This research is required not least because of the degree of separation between sexuality, family production and employment previously assumed within labour market theory. Nevertheless, this book *has* established that far from being peripheral to the labour market, or existing in some other social location, sexuality and family production do operate within the labour market, and in such a way that has far-reaching implications for understandings of the gendering of the labour market and the social construction of women's oppression. Perhaps the most significant finding is that production within the labour market has been shown not simply to be capitalist, but also patriarchal, and that (gendered) work relations contribute to the production of compulsory heterosexuality.

Notes

1 It is in fact a particular instance of the control of women's access to wages or wage-labour contracts, but it is not one which precludes them from working in the labour market or segregates women in jobs away from men. Hence it is quite distinct from the forms discussed by Hartmann and Walby (see Chapter 3).

2 Or at least not officially, and I think not often.
3 See Pateman (1988, 1989) for similar ideas.
4 But see also Tabet (1987) on prostitution in African societies.
5 See charles (1992) and Frankenberg (1993) for discussions of 'whiteness'.

References

Acker, J. (1989) 'The problem with patriarchy', *Sociology*, Vol. 23, No. 2, May, pp. 235–40.

Acker, J. (1990) 'Hierarchies, jobs and bodies: A theory of gendered organizations', *Gender and Society*, Vol. 4, No. 2, June, pp. 139–58.

Adkins, L. (1992a) Sexual work and family production: A study of the gender division of labour in the contemporary British tourist industry. Unpublished PhD thesis, Lancaster University.

Adkins, L. (1992b) 'Sexual work and the employment of women in the service industries', in M. Savage and A. Witz (eds), *Gender and Bureaucracy*. Oxford, Blackwell.

Adkins, L. and Lury, C. (1992) 'Gender and the labour market: Old theory for new?', in H. Hinds, A. Phoenix and J. Stacey (eds), *Working Out: New Directions for Women's Studies*. London, Falmer Press.

Adkins, L. and Lury, C. (1994) 'The sexual and the cultural and the gendering of the labour market', paper presented to the *Annual British Sociological Association Conference, Sexualities in Social Context*, March Preston, UK.

Alexander, P. (1988) 'Prostitution: A difficult issue for feminists', in F. Delacoste and P. Alexander (eds), *Sex Work: Writings by Women in the Sex Industry*. London, Virago.

Alfred Marks Bureau (1982) *Sex in the Office – An Investigation into the Incidence of Sexual Harassment*. London: Statistical Services Division.

Allen S. and Leonard, D. (eds) (1976) *Dependence and Exploitation in Work and Marriage*. London, Longman.

Allen, S. and Walkowitz, C. (1987) *Homeworking: Myths and Realities*. London, Macmillan.

Anderson, M. (1971) *Family Structure in Nineteenth Century Lancashire*. Cambridge, Cambridge University Press.

Bagguley, P. (1987) *Flexibility, Restructuring and Gender: Changing Employment in Britain's Hotels*, Lancaster Regionalism Group Working Paper No. 24. Lancaster, University of Lancaster.

Barron, R. D. and Norris, G. M. (1976) 'Sexual divisions in the labour market', in S. Allen and D. Leonard (eds), *Dependence and Exploitation in Work and Marriage*. London, Longman.

Barry, K. (1979) *Female Sexual Slavery*. New York, Discus.

Bart, P. (1971) 'Sexism and social science: From the gilded cage to the iron cage, or, the perils of Pauline', *Journal of Marriage and the Family*, November, pp. 734–45.

Bart, P. and O'Brien, P. (1985) *Stopping Rape: Successful Survival Strategies*. New York, Pergamon Press.

Bechhofer, F. and Elliot, B. (eds) (1981) *The Petite Bourgeoisie: Comparative Studies of the Uneasy Stratum*. London, Macmillan.

Beechey, V. (1978) 'Women and production: A critical analysis of some sociological theories of women's work', in A. Kuhn and A. Wolpe (eds), *Feminism and Materialism: Women and Modes of Production*. London, Routledge and Keegan Paul.

Beechey, V. (1982) 'Some notes on female wage labour in capitalist production', in M. Evans (ed.), *The Woman Question: Readings on the Subordination of Women*. Oxford, Oxford University Press.

Beechey, V. (1987) *Unequal Work*. London, Verso.

Beechey, V. (1988) 'Rethinking the definition of work', in J. Jenson, E. Hagen and C. Reddy (eds), *Feminization of the Labour Force: Paradoxes and Promises*. Cambridge, Polity Press.

Beechey, V. and Perkins, T. (1987) *A Matter of Hours: Women, Part-Time Work and the Labour Market*. Cambridge, Polity Press.

Bellos, A. (1991) 'Fly girls', *The Guardian*, 19–20 January, pp. 24–5.

Benet, M. (1972) *Secretary: An Enquiry into the Female Ghetto*. London, Sidgwick and Jackson.

Bertaux, D. and Bertaux-Wiame, I. (1981) 'Artisanal bakery in France: How it lives and why it survives', in F. Bechhofer and B. Elliot (eds), *The Petite Bourgeoisie: Comparative Studies of the Uneasy Stratum*. London, Macmillan.

Bland, L. (1982) '"Guardians of the race" or "vampires upon the nation's health": Female sexuality and its regulation in early twentieth century Britain', in E. Whitelegg *et al.* (eds), *The Changing Experience of Women*. Oxford, Martin Robertson.

Bourdieu, P. (1984) *Distinction: A Social Critique of the Judgement of Taste*. London, Routledge and Kegan Paul.

Bradley, H. (1989) *Men's Work, Women's Work*. Cambridge, Polity Press.

Braverman, H. (1974) *Labor and Monopoly Capital*. New York, Monthly Review Press.

Braybon, G. (1981) *Women Workers in the First World War: The British Experience*. London, Croom Helm.

British Travel Association/English Tourist Board (1993) *Tourism Intelligence Quarterly*, Vol. 15, No. 1, September. London, BTA/ETB Research Services.

Brown, C. (1984) *Black and White Britain*, Aldershot, Gower.

Bruegel, I. (1982) 'Women as a reserve army of labour: A note on the recent British experience', in E. Whitelegg *et al.* (eds), *The Changing Experience of Women*. Oxford, Martin Robertson.

Bruegel, I. (1986) 'The reserve army of labour 1974–1979', in Feminist Review (ed.), *Waged Work: A Reader*. London, Virago.

Bryan, B. *et al.* (1985) *The Heart of the Race: Black Women's Lives in Britain*. London, Virago.

Callen, H. and Ardener, S. (eds) (1984) *The Incorporated Wife*. London, Croom Helm.

Campbell, B. (1974) 'Sexuality and submission', in S. Allen, L. Sanders and J. Wallis (eds), *Conditions of Illusion*. Leeds, Feminist Books.

Cavendish, R. (1982) *On the Line*. London, Routledge and Kegan Paul.

charles, h. (1992) 'Whiteness: The relevance of politically colouring the "non"', in H. Hinds, A. Phoenix and J. Stacey (eds), *Working Out: New Directions for Women's Studies*. London, Falmer Press.

Clark, A. (1982) *Working Life of Women in the Seventeenth Century*. London, Routledge and Kegan Paul.

Cockburn, C. (1981) 'The material of male power', *Feminist Review*, No. 9, Autumn, pp. 41–58.

Cockburn, C. (1983) *Brothers: Male Dominance and Technological Change*. London, Pluto.

Cockburn, C. (1985) *Machinery of Dominance: Women, Men and Technical Know-how*. London, Pluto.

Cockburn, C. (1991) *In the Way of Women: Men's Resistance to Sex Equality in Organizations*. Basingstoke, Macmillan.

Coyle, A. (1984) *Redundant Women*. London, Women's Press.

Coyote/National Task Force on Prostitution (1988) 'Coyote/National Task Force on Prostitution', in F. Delacoste and P. Alexander, Sex-Work: *Writings by Women in the Sex Industry*. London, Virago.

Craig, C., Garnsey, E. and Rubery, J. (1985) *Payment Structures in Smaller Firms: Women's Employment in Segmented Labour Markets*, DoE Research Paper No. 48. London, Department of Employment.

Craig, C., Rubery, J., Tarling, R. and Wilkinson, F. (1982) *Labour Market Structure, Industrial Organization and Low Pay*, University of Cambridge Department of Applied Economics Occasional Paper No. 54. Cambridge, Cambridge University Press.

Crompton, R. (1986) 'Women and the service class', in R. Crompton and M. Mann (eds), *Gender and Stratification*. Cambridge, Polity Press.

Crompton, R. and Jones, G. (1984) *White Collar Proletariat: Deskilling and Gender in Clerical Work*. London, Macmillan.

Crompton, R. and Sanderson, K. (1990) *Gendered Jobs and Social Change*. London, Unwin Hyman.

Cunnison, S. (1989) 'Sex joking in the staff room', in S. Acker (ed.), *Teachers, Gender and Careers*. London, Falmer Press.

Davidoff, L. (1976) 'The rationalization of housework', in S. Allen and D. Leonard (eds), *Dependence and Exploitation in Work and Marriage*. London, Longman.

Davidoff, L. (1979) 'The separation of home and work?: Landladies and lodgers in nineteenth and twentieth century England', in S. Burman (ed.), *Fit Work for Women*. London, Croom Helm.

Davidoff, L., L'Esperance, J. and Newby, H. (1976) 'Landscape with figures', in J. Mitchell and A. Oakley (eds), *The Rights and Wrongs of Women*. Harmondsworth, Penguin.

Delacoste, F. and Alexander, P. (eds), (1988) *Sex Work: Writings by Women in the Sex Industry*. London, Virago.

Delphy, C. (1970) 'L'ennemi principal', *Partisans*, Nos 54–5, July–October. Paris, Maspero.

Delphy, C. (1984) *Close to Home: A Materialist Analysis of Women's Oppression*. London, Hutchinson.

Delphy, C. and Leonard, D. (1992) *Familiar Exploitation: A New Analysis of Marriage in Contemporary Western Societies*. Cambridge, Polity Press.

DiTomaso, N. (1989) 'Sexuality in the workplace: Discrimination and harassment', in J. Hearn, *et al.* (eds), *The Sexuality of Organization*. London, Sage.

Doeringer, P. and Piore, M. (1971) *Internal Labour Markets and Manpower Analysis*. Lexington, MA, Lexington Books.

Dronfield, L. and Soto, P. (1982) *Hardship Hotel*. London, Counter Information Services.

Edwards, R. (1979) *Contested Terrain: The Transformation of the Workplace in the Twentieth Century*. London, Heinemann.

Edwards, R., Gordon, D. and Reich, M. (1975) *Labour Market Segmentation*. Lexington, MA, Lexington Books.

Enloe, C. (1989) *Bananas, Beaches and Bases: Making Feminist Sense of International Politics*. London, Pandora.

European Network of Experts on the Situation of Women in the Labour Market (1993) *Bulletin on Women and Employment in the EC*, No. 2, April. Manchester, UMIST.

Farley, L. (1978) *Sexual Shakedown: The Sexual Harassment of Women on the Job*. New York, Warner Books.

Feminist Review Collective (ed.) (1986) *Waged Work: A Reader*. London, Virago.

Finch, J. (1983) *Married to the Job: Wives' Incorporation in Men's Work*. London, George Allen and Unwin.

Finch, J. (1989) *Family Obligations and Social Change*. Cambridge, Polity Press.

Finch, J. and Groves, D. (1983) *A Labour of Love: Women, Work and Caring*. London, Routledge and Kegan Paul.

Foucault, M. (1987) *The History of Sexuality: An Introduction*. Harmondsworth, Penguin.

Frankenberg, R. (1993) 'Growing up white: Feminism, racism and the social geography of childhood', *Feminist Review*, No. 45.

Freud, S. (1977) *On Sexuality*. Harmondsworth, Penguin.

Friedman, S. (1982) 'The Marxist paradigm: Radical feminist theorists compared', paper presented to the *British Sociological Association Annual Conference, Gender and Society*, University of Manchester, April 5–8.

Gagnon, J. and Simon, W. (1973) *Sexual Conduct: The Social Sources of Human Sexuality*. Chicago IL, Aldine.

Gamarnikow, E. (1978) 'Sexual division of labour: The case of nursing', in A. Kuhn and A. Wolpe (eds), *Feminism and Materialism: Women and Modes of Production*. London, Routledge and Kegan Paul.

Gershuny, J. and Miles, I. (1983) *The New Service Economy: The Transformation of Employment in Industrial Societies*. London, Frances Pinter.

Giobbe, E. (1990) 'Confronting the liberal lies about prostitution', in D. Leidholt and J. Raymond, (eds), *The Sexual Liberals and the Attack on Feminism*. New York, Pergamon Press.

Glendinning, C. and Millar, J. (eds) (1992) *Women and Poverty in Britain: The 1990s*. Hemel Hempstead, Harvester Wheatsheaf.

Glucksman, M. (1990) *Women Assemble: Women Workers and the New Industries in Inter-War Britain*. London, Routledge.

Goffee, R. and Scase, R. (1983) 'Class entrepreneurship and the service sector: Towards a conceptual clarification', *Service Industries Journal*, Vol. 3, pp. 146–60.

Gordon, D. (1972) *Theories of Poverty and Underemployment: Orthodox, Radical and Dual Labour Market Perspectives*. Lexington, MA, Lexington Books.

Gregory, M. (1987) 'Gender and the advertising industry', paper presented to the *Feminist Seminar Series*, Institute of Education, University of London, March.

Griffin, C. (1985) *Typical Girls?* London, Routledge and Kegan Paul.

Guerrier, Y. (1986) 'Hotel manager: An unsuitable job for a woman?', *Service Industries Journal*, Vol. 6, No. 2, pp. 227–40.

Guerrier, Y. and Lockwood, A. (1989) 'Core and peripheral employees in hotel operations', *Personnel Review*, Vol. 18, No. 1, pp. 9–15.

Guillaumin, C. (1981) 'The practice of power and belief in nature, part I: The appropriation of women', *Feminist Issues*, Vol. 1, No. 2, pp. 3–28.

Hadjifotiou, N. (1983) *Women and Harassment at Work*. London, Pluto.

Hakim, C. (1979) *Occupational Segregation: A Comparitive Study of the Degree and Pattern of the Differentiation between Men and Women's Work in Britain, the US and Other Countries*. London, Department of Employment.

Hakim, C. (1981) 'Job segregation: Trends in the 1970s', *Employment Gazette*, December, pp. 521–9.

Hamblin, A. (1974) 'The suppressed power of female sexuality', in S. Allen, L. Sanders and J. Wallis (eds), *Conditions of Illusion*. Leeds, Feminist Books.

Hamilton, C. (1912) *Marriage as a Trade*. London, Chapman and Hall.

Hanmer, J. and Maynard, M. (eds), (1987) *Women, Violence, and Social Control*. London, Macmillan.

Hanmer, J., Radford, J. and Stanko, E. (eds) (1989) *Women, Policing, and Male Violence: International Perspectives*. London, Routledge.

Hartmann, H. (1979) 'Capitalism, patriarchy and job segregation by sex', in Z. R. Eisenstein (ed.), *Capitalist Patriarchy and the Case for Socialist Feminism*. New York, Monthly Review Press.

Hartmann, H. (1981) 'The unhappy marriage of Marxism and feminism: Towards a more progressive union', in L. Sargent (ed.) *The Unhappy Marriage of Marxism and Feminism: A Debate on Class and Patriarchy*. London, Pluto.

Harvey, D. (1989) *The Condition of Postmodernity*. Oxford, Blackwell.

HCITB (1985) *Hotel and Catering Establishments in Great Britain: A Regional Analysis*, Part 1. London, HCITB.

Hearn, J. and Parkin, W. (1987) *'Sex' At 'Work': The Power and Paradox of Organisation Sexuality*. Brighton, Wheatsheaf.

Hearn, J. et al. (eds) (1989) *The Sexuality of Organization*. London, Sage.

Hochschild, A. R. (1983) *The Managed Heart: Commercialization of Human Feeling*. Berkeley, CA, University of California Press.

Holland, J., Ramazanoglu, C. and Scott, S. (1990) 'Managing risk and experiencing danger: Tensions between government AIDS education policy and young women's sexuality', *Gender and Education*, Vol. 2, No. 2, pp. 125–47.

Holly, L. (ed.) (1989) *Girls and Sexuality: Teaching and Learning*. Milton Keynes, Open University Press.

Jackson, S. (1978) 'The social context of rape: Sexual scripts and motivation', *Women's Studies International Quarterly*, Vol. 1, No. 1, pp. 27–38.

Jameson, D. (1991) *Postmodernism or the Cultural Logic of Late Capitalism*. London, Verso.

Jarvinen, M. (1993) *Of Vice and Women: Shades of Prostitution*. Oslo, Scandinavian University Press.

Jeffreys, S. (1990) *Anticlimax: A Feminist Perspective on the Sexual Revolution*. London, Women's Press.

Kanter, R. (1977) *Men and Women of the Corporation*. New York, Basic Books.

Kelly, L. (1985) 'Feminist *v* feminist: Legislating against porn in the USA, *Trouble and Strife*, No. 7, Winter, pp. 4–10.

Kelly, L. (1988) *Surviving Sexual Violence*. Cambridge, Polity Press.

Kelly, L. (1990) 'Abuse in the making: The production and use of pornography', *Trouble and Strife*, No. 19, Summer, pp. 32–37.

Koedt, A. (1970) 'The myth of the vaginal orgasm', in L. Tanner (ed.), *Voices from Women's Liberation*. New York, Signet.

Landry, C., Montgomery, J., Worpole, K., Gratton, C. and Murray, R. (1989) *The Last Resort: Tourism. Tourist Employment and Post-Tourism in the South East*. London, Comedia.

Lash, S. (1990) *Sociology of Postmodernism*. London, Routledge.

Lash, S. and Urry, J. (1987) *The End of Organized Capitalism*. Cambridge, Polity Press.

Laws, S. (1990) *Issues of Blood: The Politics of Menstruation*. London, Macmillan.

Leeds TUCRIC (1983) *Sexual Harassment of Women at Work*. Leeds, TUCRIC.

Lees, S. (1986) *Losing Out: Sexuality and Adolescent Girls*. London, Hutchinson.

Lees, S. (1993) *Sugar and Spice: Sexuality and Adolescent Girls*. Harmondsworth, Penguin.

Leonard, D. (1980) *Sex and Generation: A Study of Courtship and Weddings*. London, Tavistock.

Leonard, D. (1984) 'The origin of the family, private property and socialist feminism?', *Trouble and Strife*, No. 3, Summer, pp. 39–43.

Leonardo, M. di (1987) 'The female world of cards and holidays: Women, families and the work of kinship', *Signs*, Vol. 12, No. 3, pp. 440–53.

Llewellyn, C. (1981) 'Occupational mobility and the use of the comparative method', in H. Roberts (ed.), *Doing Feminist Research*. London, Routledge.

Lopez-Jones, N. (1988) 'Workers: Introducing the English Collective of Prostitutes', in F. Delacoste and P. Alexander, *Sex-Work: Writings by Women in the Sex Industry*. London, Virago.

Lyndon, S. (1970) 'The politics of orgasm', in R. Morgan (ed.), *Sisterhood is Powerful: An Anthology of Writings from the Women's Liberation Movement*. New York, Vantage.

MacKinnon, C. (1979) *Sexual Harassment of Working Women.* New Haven, CT, Yale University Press.

MacKinnon, C. (1982) 'Feminism, Marxism, method, and the state: An agenda for theory', *Signs*, Vol. 7, No. 3, pp. 515–44.

MacKinnon, C. (1983) 'Feminism, Marxism, method, and the state: Toward feminist jurisprudence', *Signs*, Vol. 8, No. 4, pp. 635-58.

MacKinnon, C. (1987) *Feminism Unmodified: Discourses on Life and Law.* Cambridge, MA, Harvard University Press.

MacKinnon, C. (1989) *Towards a Feminist Theory of the State.* Cambridge, MA, Harvard University Press.

Mahony, P. (1985) *Schools for Boys? Co-education Reassessed.* London, Hutchinson.

Maitland, S. (1991) 'Lipstick traces, egg on their faces', *The Observer*, 18 August.

Marcuse, H. (1969) *Eros and Civilization.* London, Sphere.

Mark-Lawson, J. and Witz, A. (1986) *From 'Family Labour' To 'Family Wage': The Case of 19th Century Women's Labour in Coalmining,* Lancaster Regionalism Group Working Paper No. 18. Lancaster, University of Lancaster.

Marshall, J. (1984) *Women Managers: Travellers in a Man's World.* Chichester, John Wiley.

Martin, J. and Roberts, C. (1984) *Women and Employment: A Lifetime Perspective.* London, HMSO.

McDowell, L. (1991) 'Life without father and ford: The new gender order of post-fordism', *Transactions of British Geographers*, Vol. 16, No. 4, pp. 400–419.

McLeod, E. (1982) *Women Working: Prostitution Now.* London, Croom Helm.

McNally, F. (1979) *Women for Hire: A Study of the Female Office Worker.* London, Macmillan.

Meissner, M. *et al.* (1988) 'No exit for wives: Sexual division of labour and the cumulation of household demands in Canada', in R. Pahl (ed.), *On Work: Historical, Comparative and Theoretical Approaches.* Oxford, Blackwell.

Mies, M. (1986) *Patriarchy and Accumulation on a World Scale.* London, Zed.

Milkman, R. (1976) 'Women's work and economic crisis: Some lessons of the great depression', *Review of Radical Political Economy*, Vol. 8, No. 1, pp. 73–97.

Minge, W. (1986) 'The industrial revolution and European family: "Childhood" as a market for family labour', in E. Leacock and H. I. Safa (eds), *Women's Work: Development and the Division of Labour by Gender.* South Hadley MASS, Bergin and Garvey.

Mitchell, J. (1975) *Psychoanalysis and Feminism*. Harmondsworth, Penguin.

Mitter, S. (1986) *Common-Fate, Common Bond: Women in the Global Economy*. London, Pluto.

Morgan, R. (ed.) (1970) *Sisterhood is Powerful: An Anthology of Writings from the Women's Liberation Movement*. New York, Vantage.

Morris, L. (1990) *The Workings of the Household*. Cambridge, Polity Press.

Newby, H., Rose, D., Saunders, P. and Bell, C. (1981) 'Farming for survival: The small farmer in the contemporary rural class structure', in F. Bechhofer and B. Elliot (eds), *The Petite Bourgeoisie: Comparative Studies of the Uneasy Stratum*. London, Macmillan.

Oakley, A. (1981) *Subject Woman*. Oxford, Martin Robertson.

Offe, C. (1985) *Disorganized Capitalism: Contemporary Transformations of Work and Politics*. Cambridge, Polity Press.

Office of Population Censuses and Surveys (1981). *Census of Population*. London, HMSO.

Partington, G. (1976) *Women Teachers in the Twentieth Century in England and Wales*. Windsor, NFER.

Pateman, C. (1988) *The Sexual Contract*. Cambridge, Polity Press.

Pateman, C. (1989), The Disorder of Women: Democracy, Feminism and Political Theory. Cambridge, Polity Press.

Phillips, A. and Taylor, B. (1986) 'Sex and skill', in Feminist Review (ed.), *Waged Work: A Reader*. London, Virago.

Phizacklea, A. (1988a) 'Gender, racism and occupational segregation', in S. Walby (ed.), *Gender Segregation at Work*. Milton Keynes, Open University Press.

Phizacklea, A. (1988b) 'Entrepreneurship, ethnicity and gender', in S. Westwood and P. Bhachu (eds), *Enterprising Women: Ethnicity, Economy and Gender Relations*. London, Routledge.

Phizacklea, A. (1990) *Unpacking the Fashion Industry*. London, Routledge.

Plummer, K. (1975) *Sexual Stigma: An Interactionist Account*. London, Routledge.

Pollert, A. (1981) *Girls, Wives, Factory Lives*. London, Macmillan.

Porter, M. (1983) *Home, Work and Class Consciousness*. Manchester, Manchester University Press.

Pringle, R. (1988a) *Secretaries' Talk: Sexuality, Power, and Work*. London, Verso.

Pringle, R. (1989b) 'Bureaucracy, rationality and sexuality: The case of secretaries', in J. Hearn, D. L. Sheppard, P. Tancred-Sherrif and G. Burrel (eds), *The Sexuality of Organization*. London, Sage.

Purcell, K. (1991) 'Gender and the experience of employment', in G. Esland (ed.), *Education, Training and Employment*. Wokingham, Addison-Wesley.

Rajan, A. (1897) *The Second Industrial Revolution?: Businesses and Jobs Outlook for UK Growth Industries*. London, Butterworth.

Raymond, J. (1986) *A Passion for Friends: Toward a Philosophy of Female Affection*. London, Women's Press.

Rees, T. (1992) *Women and the Labour Market*. London, Routledge.

Reich, W. (1969) *The Sexual Revolution*. New York, Farrar, Strauss and Giroux.

Rich, A. (1983) 'Compulsory heterosexuality and lesbian existence', in A. Snitow, C. Stansell and S. Thompson (eds), *Powers of Desire: The Politics of Sexuality*. New York, Monthly Review Press.

Rose, J. (1983) 'Femininity and its discontents', *Feminist Review*, No. 14, Summer, pp. 5–21.

Rubery, J. (1978) 'Structured labour markets, worker organization and low pay', *Cambridge Journal of Economics*, No. 2, pp. 17–36.

Rubin, L. (1979) 'The marriage bed', in E. Shapiro and B. Shapiro (eds), *The Women Say, The Men Say: Issues in Politics, Work, Family, Sexuality, Power*. New York, Delta.

Russell, D. (1982) *Rape in Marriage*. New York, Macmillan.

Russell, D. (1984) *Sexual Exploitation: Rape, Child Sexual Abuse, and Workplace Harassment*. London, Sage.

Russell, D. and Howell, N. (1983) 'The prevalence of rape in the US revisited', *Signs*, Vol. 8, No. 4, pp. 688–93.

Savage, M. (1982) *Control at Work: North Lancashire Cotton Weaving, 1890–1940*, Lancaster Regionalism Group Working Paper No. 7. University of Lancaster.

Savage, M. and Witz, A. (eds) (1992) *Gender and Bureaucracy*. Oxford, Blackwell.

Sayers, J. (1986) *Sexual Contradictions: Psychology, Psychoanalysis and Feminism*. London, Tavistock.

Scase, R. and Goffee, R. (1980a) *The Real World of the Small Business Owner*. London, Croom Helm.

Scase, R. and Goffee, R. (1980b) 'Home life in a small business', *New Society*, October, pp. 220–22.

Scott, A. (1986) 'Industrialization, gender segregation and stratification theory', in R. Crompton and M. Mann (eds), *Gender and Stratification*. Cambridge, Polity Press.

Segal, L. (1987) *Is the Future Female?: Troubled Thoughts on Contemporary Feminism*. London, Virago.

Segal, L. and McIntosh, M. (eds) (1992) *Sex Exposed: Sexuality and the Pornography Debate*. London, Virago.

Shaw, J. (1981) 'Family, state and compulsory education', Unit 13, Open University Course E353, *Society, Education and the State*. Milton Keynes, Open University Press.

Smelser, N. (1959) *Social Change in the Industrial Revolution: An*

Application of Theory to the Lancashire Cotton Industry, 1770–1840. London, Routledge.

Smith, A. D. (1986) 'Miscellaneous Services', in A. D. Smith (ed.), *Commercial Service Industries*. Aldershot, Gower.

Spradley, J. and Mann, B. (1975) *The Cocktail Waitress: Woman's Work in a Man's World*. New York, John Wiley.

Stanko, E. (1985) *Intimate Intrusions: Women's Experience of Male Violence*. London, Routledge and Kegan Paul.

Stanko, E. (1988) 'Keeping women in and out of line: Sexual harassment and occupational segregation', in S. Walby (ed.), *Gender Segregation at Work*. Milton Keynes, Open University Press.

Stanko, E. (1990) *Everyday Violence: How Women and Men Experience Sexual and Physical Violence*. London, Pandora.

Summerfield, P. (1984) *Women Workers in the Second World War*. London, Croom Helm.

Tabet, P. (1985) 'Fertile naturelle, reproduction forcee' ('Natural fertility, forced reproduction'), in N.-C. Mathieu (ed.), *L'Arraisonnement des Femmes: Essais an Anthropologie des Sexes*. Paris, Editions de l'Ecole de Hautes Etudes en Sciences Sociales.

Tabet, P. (1987) 'Du don au tarif' ('From gift to fee'), *Les Temps Modernes*, No. 490, May, pp. 1–53.

Tabet, P. (1989) 'I'm the meat, I'm the knife: Sexual service, migration and repression in some African societies', in G. Pheterson (ed.), *A Vindication of the Rights of Whores*. Seattle, WA, Seal Press.

Thoen, T. and Kristianson, N. (1989) 'Jeux sans frontieres: International campaigns against sex-tourism', *Trouble and Strife*, No. 16, Summer, pp. 10–13.

Truong, T.-D. (1990) *Sex, Money and Morality: Prostitution and Tourism in South-East Asia*. London, Zed.

Urry, J. (1986) *Services: Some Issues of Analysis*, Lancaster Regionalism Group Working Paper No. 17. Lancaster, University of Lancaster.

Urry, J. (1990) *The Tourist Gaze: Leisure and Travel in Contemporary Societies*. London, Sage.

Valverde, M. (1989) 'Beyond gender dangers and private pleasures: Theory and ethics in the sex debates', *Feminist Studies*, Vo. 15, No. 2, pp. 237–54.

Vance, C. (ed.) (1984) *Pleasure and Danger: Exploring Female Sexuality*. London, Routledge and Kegan Paul.

Wajcman, J. (1983) *Women in Control*. Milton Keynes, Open University Press.

Walby, S. (1986) *Patriarchy at Work: Patriarchal and Capitalist Relations in Employment*. Cambridge, Polity Press.

Walby, S. (ed.) (1988) *Gender Segregation at Work*. Milton Keynes, Open University Press.

Walby, S. (1990) *Theorizing Patriarchy*. Oxford, Blackwell.

Walker, R. (1985) 'Is there a service economy?: The changing capitalist division of labour', *Science and Society*, Vol. XLIX, No. 1, Spring, pp. 42–83.

Ware, V. (1992) *Beyond the Pale: White Women, Racism and History*. London, Verso.

Weeks, J. (1981) *Sex, Politics and Society: The Regulation of Sexuality Since 1800*. London, Longman.

Westwood, S. (1984) *All Day, Every Day: Factory and Family in the Making of Women's Lives*. London, Pluto.

Westwood, S. and Bhachu, P. (1988) *Enterprising Women: Ethnicity, Economy and Gender Relations*. London, Routledge.

Whiting, P. (1972) 'Female sexuality: Its political implications', in M. Wandor (ed.), *The Body Politic: Writings from the Women's Liberation Movement in Britain 1969–1972*. London, Stage One.

Williams, C. (1988) *Blue, White and Pink Collar Workers: Technicians, Bank Employees and Flight Attendants*. London, Allen and Unwin.

Wittig, M. (1982), 'The Category of Sex', *Feminist Issues (2)* 2, 63–68.

Wittig, M. (1989) 'On the social contract', in A. van Kooten Niekerk and T. van der Meer (eds), *Which Homosexuality?: Essays from the International Scientific Conference on Lesbian and Gay Studies*. London, GMP.

Witz, A. (1988) 'Patriarchal relations and patterns of sex segregation in the medical division of labour', in S. Walby (ed.), *Gender Segregation at Work*. Milton Keynes, Open University Press.

Wood, J. (1984), 'Groping towards sexism: Boys' sex talk', in A. McRobbie and M. Nava (eds), *Gender and Generation*. London, Macmillan.

Woolf, N. (1990) *The Beauty Myth*. London, Chatto and Windus.

Yuval-Davis, N. and Anthias, F. (eds) (1989) *Woman–Nation–State*. London, Macmillan.

Index

MOTHERHOOD AND MODERNITY
AN INVESTIGATION INTO THE RATIONAL DIMENSI⟨ ⟩ OF MOTHERING

Christine Everingham

This book takes a central topic in women's studies and sociolog⟨ ⟩ family and presents an innovative analysis linking motherh⟨ ⟩ broader sociological debates on modernity, rationality and individ⟨ ⟩ It has many strengths, including a well handled mix of theoret⟨ ⟩ ethnographic material, a focused review of contemporary discus⟨ ⟩ rationality and the self, an excellent review of the literature on mo⟨ ⟩ and morality, and perhaps most importantly, an insightful and il⟨ ⟩ ting central hypothesis which will promote lively debate.

Current models of mothering are based on the assumption that⟨ ⟩ have biologically determined 'needs' that mothers learn to recogr⟨ ⟩ meet in socially approved ways. Christine Everingham deve⟨ ⟩ alternative model of nurturing that locates mothers as subjects, ⟨ ⟩ constructing the perspective of their child while asserting their ow⟨ ⟩ and interests in a particular socio-cultural context. This powerf⟨ ⟩ extends contemporary scholarly debates on mothering and mo⟨ ⟩ and is a valuable resource for teaching in women's studies and soc⟨ ⟩

Contents

168pp   0 335 19195 9 (Paperback)   0 335 19196 7 (Hardl⟨ ⟩

THE MAKING OF MEN
MASCULINITIES, SEXUALITIES AND SCHOOLING

Máirtín Mac an Ghaill

Wayne: 'You can't trust girls because of what they expect from you... And you can't be honest with your mates because they'll probably tell other people.'

Rajinder: 'There's a lot of sexuality... African Caribbeans are seen as better at football ... and dancing ... the white kids and Asians are jealous because they think the girls will really prefer the black kids.'

Richard: 'Okay sharing the housework and things like that are fair. But it's all the stuff not making girls sex objects. It's ridiculous. What are you supposed to do. Become gay?'

William: 'We wanked each other one night when we were really drunk. Then later on when I saw him, he said he had a girlfriend. I knew he hadn't. We just had to move apart because we got too close.'

Gilroy: 'It's the girls who have all the power. Like they have the choice and can make you look a prat in front of your mates.'

Joanne: 'You lot are obsessed with your knobs ... all your talk is crap. It's just to prove you're better than your mates. Why don't you all get together and measure your little plonkers?'

Frank: 'My dad spends all his time in the pub with his mates. Why doesn't he want to be with me? Why doesn't he say he loves me?... It does my head in.'

Máirtín Mac an Ghaill explores how boys learn to be men in schools whilst policing their own and others' sexualities. He focuses upon the students' confusions and contradictions in their gendered experiences; and upon how schools actively produce, through the official and hidden curriculum, a range of masculinities which young men come to inhabit. He does full justice to the complex phenomenon of male heterosexual subjectivities and to the role of schooling in forming sexual identities.

Contents

224pp   0 335 15781 5 (Paperback)   0 335 15782 3 (Hardback)

ST. JOHN FISHER COLLEGE LIBRARY

0 1220 0029132 0

THE MODERN GIRL
GIRLHOOD AND GROWING UP

Lesley Johnson

In the early 1960s, Betty Friedan made a plea for women to grow up, to become – in her terms – fully developed persons. In doing so she placed the question 'What does it mean to grow up as a woman?' at the heart of debates about the project of contemporary feminism. Feminist theory in recent years has been concerned to rethink how the experience of growing up and adult womanhood should be defined. In *The Modern Girl* Lesley Johnson looks at the 1950s and early 1960s in Australia as a period in which the girlhood and growing up as young women was being transformed in major ways. Through an investigation of such figures as the modern schoolgirl, the adolescent, the juvenile delinquent and the teenage girl of this era, she points to at least some of the reasons why many women would find Friedan's call so powerful. She uses this analysis to argue that there are dangers in the way contemporary feminism continues to look for satisfactory definitions of adult womanhood.

The Modern Girl draws on and makes a valuable contribution to debates within feminist cultural studies about women and modernity, the historically changing nature of female subjectivity and about the project of feminism today.

Contents

Introduction – Feminism and the 'awakening of women' – The importance of having: modernity, women and consumerism – Growing up as a modern individual: on youth and modernity in the 1950s – Growing up in modern Australia: the study of young people in Australia in the 1950s – The modern school girl: debates about the education of young women – Youth on the streets: the social regulation of young people as 'teenagers' and as 'youth' – 'The best of everything': defining the space of the teenage girl – Endings – Notes – Bibliography – Index.

192pp   0 335 09998 X (Paperback)   0 335 09999 8 (Hardback)

HD 6060.5 .G7 A34 1995
Adkins, Lisa, 1966-
Gendered work

AAY-5244